PERFECT

FRUIT

DESSERTS

P·E·R·F·E·C·T
FRUIT
D E S S E R T S

DORLING KINDERSLEY
LONDON • NEW YORK • SYDNEY • MOSCOW

A DORLING KINDERSLEY BOOK

Created and Produced by
CARROLL & BROWN LIMITED
5 Lonsdale Road
London NW6 6RA

Editorial Director Jeni Wright
Editors Jennifer Feller
Norma MacMillan
Sally Poole
Stella Vayne
Assisted by Joanna Pitchfork

Art Editor Vicky Zentner
Designers Lucy De Rosa
Lyndel Donaldson
Wendy Rogers
Mary Staples
Lisa Webb

First published in Great Britain in 1997
by Dorling Kindersley Limited
9 Henrietta Street, London WC2E 8PS

Previously published in 1992 under the title
Look & Cook Fruit Desserts

A CIP catalogue record for this book is available
from the British Library

ISBN 0-7513-0492-1

Reproduced by Colourscan, Singapore
Printed and bound in Singapore by Star Standard

CONTENTS

PERFECT FRUIT DESSERTS

Welcome to **Perfect Fruit Desserts.** This volume is designed to be the simplest, most informative cookbook you'll ever own. It is the closest I can come to sharing my techniques for cooking my favourite recipes without actually being with you in the kitchen looking over your shoulder.

EQUIPMENT

Equipment and ingredients often determine whether or not you can cook a particular dish, so **Perfect Fruit Desserts** illustrates everything you need at the beginning of each recipe. You'll see at a glance how long a recipe takes to cook, how many servings it makes, what the finished dish looks like, and how much preparation can be done ahead. When you start to cook, you'll find the preparation and cooking are organized into easy-to-follow steps. Each stage is colour-coded and everything is shown in photographs with brief text to go with each step. You will never be in doubt about what it is you are doing, why you are doing it, or how it should look.

INGREDIENTS

🍽 SERVES 6 🥣 WORK TIME 30–35 MINUTES 🍴 COOKING TIME 25–35 MINUTES

I've also included helpful hints and ideas under "Anne Says". These may list an alternative ingredient or piece of equipment, or sometimes the reason for using a certain method is explained, or there is advice on mastering a particular technique. Similarly, if there is a crucial stage in a recipe when things can go wrong, I've included some warnings called "Take Care".

Many of the photographs are annotated to pinpoint why certain pieces of equipment work best, or how the food should look at that stage of cooking. Because presentation is so important, a picture of the finished dish and serving suggestions are at the end of each recipe.

Thanks to all this information, you can't go wrong. I'll be with you every step of the way. So please, come with me into the kitchen to look, cook, and create some exciting **Perfect Fruit Desserts.**

WHY FRUIT?

There is nothing better than fresh, sun-ripened fruit – except, of course, a luscious dessert made from them. The vibrant colours of limes, cherries, peaches, and plums, among others, are lovely to look at – and even better to eat! Whether in a simple salad, or a festive flambé, whether served hot or chilled, fruit is the basis for an unlimited range of dinner finales.

RECIPE CHOICE

Everyone has a favourite fruit dessert, whether it's a tangy lemon soufflé or an exotic Pavlova, the French tarte Tatin, or blackberry fool – an English summer treat. Here you'll find cold desserts ranging from unusual fruit salads to grand soufflés, as well as hot desserts such as fritters and flambéed pineapple, with a selection of pies, tarts, and pastries to tempt even the faintest appetite.

COLD DESSERTS

Strawberry Shortcakes: crumbly shortcakes are filled with luscious strawberries and Chantilly cream, with a pool of fresh strawberry coulis all around. *Lemon Shortcakes with Blueberries:* a hint of lemon flavours the shortcakes, which are filled with plump blueberries and cream. *Pavlova with Tropical Fruit:* kiwi, pineapple, and mango give a tropical lilt to this giant meringue puff. *Pavlova with Mixed Berries:* this classic duo of meringue and fresh berries was created for the famed ballerina. *Summer Fruit Salad:* a decorative watermelon basket holds peaches, nectarines, cherries, melon, and assorted berries. *Exotic Fruit Salad:* chunks of pineapple, papaya, star fruit, kiwi, mango, and lychees are spiked with white wine and rum and jewelled with pomegranate seeds. *Apricot Mousse:* the delicately perfumed mousse of golden apricots is decorated with rosettes of Chantilly cream – superlative! *Strawberry Mousse with Fresh Plum Sauce:* purple plum sauce makes a striking complement for strawberry mousse. *Cold Lemon Soufflé:* fluffy lemon soufflé is topped with strips of candied lemon zest – a fitting end to a grand dinner. *Individual Cold Lime Soufflés:* the tang of lime lightens these chilled miniature soufflés.

Pear and Redcurrant Compote: blackcurrant liqueur and redcurrants add punch to poached pears. *Nectarine Compote:* cardamom and pistachios give poached nectarines a Middle Eastern touch. *Dried Fruit Compote:* this winter fruit dessert has orange zest and rum flavouring. *Poires Belle Hélène:* poached pears and homemade vanilla ice cream are coated with rich chocolate sauce. *Poached Pear Fans with Chocolate Sauce:* stylish presentation of pears in a pool of cream and chocolate sauce. *Mango Sorbet:* refreshing ice has the rich flavour of ripe mango. *Melon Sorbet:* aromatic cantaloupe or honeydew melon sums up the taste of summer. *Lemon Sorbet:* served in the hollowed-out lemon shells, zesty sorbet delights children and adults alike. *Orange Caramel Creams:* agreeably tart version of caramel custard is garnished with fresh orange. *Lime Caramel Creams:* the tangy flavour of lime blends deliciously with a light caramel sauce. *Raspberry Bavarian Cake:* rich and elegant cake has fresh raspberry Bavarian cream sandwiched between layers of sponge cake. *Orange Bavarian Cake:* orange and Grand Marnier enliven the creamy Bavarian filling in this dessert, to be enjoyed year-round. *Blackberry Fool:* puréed fresh blackberries, smooth pastry cream, and whipped cream make a combination to enchant us all. *Rhubarb Fool:* refreshingly tart rhubarb with a sweet cream base has a finishing touch of stem ginger. *Redcurrant Fool:* a great way to use a tricky fruit.

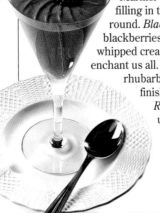

HOT DESSERTS

Baked Peaches with Amaretti: a northern Italian classic fills sweet peaches with crushed almond-flavoured biscuits. *Baked Figs with Amaretti:* ripe figs are stuffed to serve with orange-flavoured Chantilly cream. *Raspberry Soufflé Puddings with Kirsch Custard Sauce:* an individual version of the French classic, this is made with fresh berries. *Strawberry Soufflé Pudding with Mint Custard Sauce:* puréed strawberries are folded into meringue and baked – simple yet divine! *Fruit Fritters in Beer Batter with Fresh Orange Sauce:* light batter coats slices of pineapple, apple, and banana. *Fruit Fritters in Champagne Batter with Raspberry Coulis:* fritters sparkle with an effervescent Champagne batter coating.
Caribbean Flambéed Pineapple: tropical treat has rings of pineapple, sautéed with brown sugar, pecans, and rum, topped with toasted coconut. *Flambéed Bananas Foster:* this New Orleans classic combines bananas, plump raisins, cinnamon, and dark rum finished with sugar-glazed almonds. *Cherries Jubilee:* black cherries are flambéed with kirsch and served with vanilla ice cream. *Gratin of Fresh Berries with Sabayon:* fresh mixed berries are topped with fluffy sabayon sauce and briefly grilled. *Berries and Ice Cream with Sabayon:* the unbeatable combination of berries and ice cream heats up when topped with sabayon sauce and quickly glazed. *Gratin of Citrus Fruit and Grapes with Sabayon:* segments of orange and grapefruit with firm grapes make a pretty winter gratin.

PIES, TARTS, AND PASTRIES

Peach Pie: baked peaches make a juicy filling, topped with a pastry lattice. *Cherry Pie:* the most famous of all American pies, made with fresh cherries, needs no introduction. *Normandy Pear Tart:* a pretty flower-shaped design of pear slices adorns this regional French tart, filled with almond cream. *Normandy Peach Tart:* fresh peaches take the place of pears, with a jam glaze. *Phyllo Apricot Turnovers:* triangles of phyllo enclose little bites of apricot spiced with cinnamon, nutmeg, and cloves. *Phyllo Apricot Purses:* aromatic apricot filling is wrapped in squares of phyllo, shaped like purses. *Phyllo Berry Turnovers:* lightly sweetened berries fill crisp pastry turnovers. *Caramelized Upside-Down Apple Tart:* firm apples are cooked in caramel and served on a pastry crust, with homemade crème fraîche. *Caramelized Upside-Down Pear Tart:* juice from pear halves combines with caramel to make a delicious topping. *Fresh Fruit Tartlets:* colourful fresh fruit are displayed in individual pastry shells lined with pastry cream. *Fresh Fruit Tart:* a full-size tart is filled with fresh fruit, arranged in concentric circles, glistening with jam glaze. *Cherry Strudel:* layers of flaky pastry surround fresh cherries, walnuts, brown sugar, and cinnamon in this Austrian favourite. *Dried Fruit Strudel:* rum-soaked dried fruit and walnuts are the filling for strudel dough, served with a Chantilly cream accompaniment. *Hazelnut Torte with Strawberries:* a three-layer castle of golden brown hazelnut pastry has strawberry and fluffy Chantilly cream filling, plus a raspberry coulis. *Almond Torte with Peaches:* peach slices and whipped cream are layered with almond pastry – a knockout!

EQUIPMENT

Given the wide range of fruit available, and the different methods of preparing them, a variety of equipment is needed. Happily, only a few items are specialized, and in almost all cases just standard kitchen tools are required.

A chef's knife is always the best to use for slicing or cutting up fruit, particularly when it is large. Small knives come in handy for berries and small-to-medium-sized fruit. The acid in most fruit will discolour a carbon steel blade, so always use a stainless steel serrated knife or a regular blade with a high stainless content. All knives should be sharpened regularly and stored carefully to prevent dulling. The type of peeler you prefer, whether with a fixed or swivel blade, is up to you. The few special tools for cleaning and shaping fruit that you will need include a melon baller and a cherry stoner. It is also useful to have a grapefruit knife with a curved serrated blade for hollowing many small fruit.

Pie and cake tins are needed for the pies, tarts, and tortes here. It is not advisable to change the size of the tin called for in a recipe because the pastry quantity given will be wrong or the cake mixture will not bake correctly. A springform tin is required for the Bavarian cake, and ramekins are needed for individual soufflés and fruit-flavoured caramel creams.

Another useful piece of equipment for fruit desserts is a whisk, preferably a balloon whisk that will incorporate maximum air into whipped cream, egg whites, or sabayon sauce. For whisking egg whites, a copper bowl and balloon whisk are the classic French utensils. An electric mixer can almost always be substituted.

For piping decorations, a piping bag with a selection of different nozzles is necessary, and you will need an ice-cream maker for sorbets and any desserts with ice cream as accompaniment. At the other end of the spectrum, a deep-fat fryer is required to cook the fritters.

INGREDIENTS

Many ingredients complement fruit. A sprinkling of sugar brings out the best flavour, while a squeeze of lemon juice adds a pleasant tartness, with the added benefit of preventing fruit such as peaches and pears from discolouring. Further intensity of flavour can be added by a wide assortment of alcoholic spirits and liqueurs, such as rum, crème de cassis, and amaretto: they add that certain "something" when poaching, soaking, and flambéing.

Whipped and Chantilly cream pair happily with almost all fruit, adding richness and a contrast of colour. An alternative is pastry cream, made with milk, egg yolks, sugar, and a thickening of flour, used as a background in fruit tarts and to lighten fruit purées.

Chocolate combines luxuriously with a broad range of fruit, while gelatine is indispensable for shaping many moulded desserts. As for herb sprigs and spices, they turn up in surprising places, flavouring poaching liquids and sorbets, and adding fragrance to purées. Herbs also provide a touch of fresh green decoration.

TECHNIQUES

The wide variety of fruit calls for specific techniques to deal with each one. Stone fruit is often peeled and stoned, especially in presentations calling for fruit halves and slices. The fruit is briefly scalded to loosen the skin before it is halved to remove the stone. Other fruit, such as pears and apples, need only to be peeled with a vegetable peeler before being cut into halves and/or slices.

Citrus fruit are prepared differently. The juice is often squeezed out or the fruit is peeled with a knife and then cut into segments. Zest from citrus fruit may be grated to use as a flavouring or cut into strips and candied for decoration.

Tropical fruit, such as pineapple and mango, require individual treatment. Pineapple is peeled with a large knife to remove the skin and "eyes", while mango flesh is sliced off the stone, then scored into cubes before being cut from the skin.

Both raw and cooked fruit may be puréed to act as the foundation of a recipe or as the accompanying sauce. The techniques for cooking fruit – poaching, baking, and so on – are clearly explained here, as is the important point of judging just when fruit is done: tender but not mushy.

As with the other volumes in this series, there are many techniques for preparing other ingredients. For example, you will find how to use a vanilla pod; how to make Chantilly cream; how to make pastry leaves; how to make fruit jam glaze; how to fold mixtures together; how to stiffly whisk egg whites; how to make crème fraîche; and how to fill a piping bag and pipe rosettes.

STRAWBERRY SHORTCAKES

🍽 SERVES 6   🥄 WORK TIME 15-20 MINUTES   🍲 BAKING TIME 12-15 MINUTES

EQUIPMENT

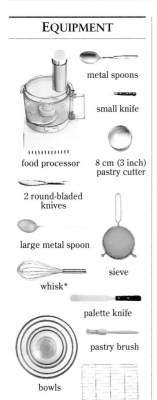

metal spoons

small knife

8 cm (3 inch) pastry cutter

food processor

2 round-bladed knives

large metal spoon

sieve

whisk*

palette knife

pastry brush

bowls

wire rack

serrated knife

chopping board

baking sheet

*electric mixer can also be used

Real strawberry shortcake is made with a scone-like dough, like this rich version. A tangy strawberry coulis mingles well with the shortcakes and cream.

GETTING AHEAD

Shortcakes should be eaten the day of baking and are best eaten fresh from the oven. Make the Chantilly cream not more than 2 hours ahead, and assemble the shortcakes just before serving.

INGREDIENTS

strawberries

double cream

unsalted butter

kirsch (optional)

vanilla essence

plain flour

baking powder

caster sugar

icing sugar

metric	SHOPPING LIST	imperial
500 g	strawberries	1 lb
45 g	caster sugar	1 1/2 oz
	For the shortcakes	
60 g	unsalted butter, more for baking sheet	2 oz
250 g	plain flour	8 oz
15 ml	baking powder	1 tbsp
2.5 ml	salt	1/2 tsp
45 g	caster sugar	1 1/2 oz
175 ml	double cream, more if needed	6 fl oz
	For the strawberry coulis	
500 g	strawberries	1 lb
30-45 ml	icing sugar	2-3 tbsp
30 ml	kirsch (optional)	2 tbsp
	For the Chantilly cream	
250 ml	double cream	8 fl oz
30-45 ml	caster sugar	2-3 tbsp
5 ml	vanilla essence	1 tsp

ORDER OF WORK

1 PREPARE AND BAKE THE SHORTCAKES

2 PREPARE THE STRAWBERRIES AND CHANTILLY CREAM

3 ASSEMBLE THE SHORTCAKES

1 PREPARE AND BAKE THE SHORTCAKES

1 Heat the oven to 220°C (425°F, Gas 7). Butter the baking sheet.

Make well in dry ingredients with your fingers

2 Sift the flour into a large bowl with the baking powder, salt, and caster sugar and make a well in the centre.

3 Cut the butter into pieces and add to the well.

Cut with knives in scissor fashion

4 Cut the butter into the flour mixture using the 2 knives.

Cool fingers ensure dough will not be sticky

Lifting mixture while rubbing results in light pastry

5 Rub the mixture with your fingertips, lifting and crumbling to aerate it, until it forms fine crumbs.

6 Make a well in the centre, add the cream, and toss quickly with the palette knife to form crumbs. Add a little more cream if the mixture seems dry.

! TAKE CARE !
Do not overmix or the shortcakes will be heavy.

7 Press all of the crumbs together with your hands to form a rough ball of dough.

8 Turn the dough onto a floured surface and knead lightly for a few seconds – the dough should remain quite rough. Pat the dough out to a round 1 cm (¹/₂ inch) thick.

Light, firm pressure extends dough quickly

Flour your hands if necessary

Evenly space rounds on baking sheet to allow for expansion

9 Cut out rounds with the pastry cutter. Pat out the trimmings and cut additional rounds, for a total of 6 rounds. Transfer to the prepared baking sheet.

Cut rounds as close together as possible to obtain maximum number of rounds

ANNE SAYS
"You will probably have some dough left over. If you don't want to waste any dough, cut it into triangles rather than rounds, although this isn't traditional."

10 Bake the shortcakes in the heated oven until very lightly browned, 12-15 minutes. Transfer them to the wire rack to cool.

HOW TO MAKE A BERRY COULIS

A coulis is a sauce of thickish consistency. Some of the best coulis are made with fresh berries; frozen berries can be substituted but they lack the perfume and flavour of fresh ones.

1 Hull and pick over the berries, washing them only if they are dirty. Purée the berries in a food processor or blender.

2 Transfer to a bowl. Stir in icing sugar to taste and liqueur, if you like.

3 For raspberries, work the puréed fruit through a fine sieve to remove the pips. The finished coulis should be thick enough to coat the spoon.

2 PREPARE THE STRAWBERRIES AND CHANTILLY CREAM

1 Hull the strawberries and cut into slices, reserving 6 small whole berries with hulls for garnish.

Use small knife to hull and slice strawberries

2 Sprinkle the sliced strawberries with the caster sugar and let stand to soften, 5-10 minutes. Make a berry coulis with the strawberries, icing sugar, and the kirsch, if you like (see box, left).

Make neat cuts in berry halves

3 Halve the reserved whole strawberries lengthwise, then slice just to the hull so that the halves remain intact. Press each half flat into a fan with your thumb. Make the Chantilly cream, flavouring it with the vanilla essence (see box, page 14).

HOW TO MAKE CHANTILLY CREAM

Chantilly cream is whipped cream flavoured with sugar and vanilla, brandy, rum, or a liqueur such as Grand Marnier. Double cream (with minimum 48% fat) is best for Chantilly cream, and it should be thoroughly chilled. Chantilly cream can be kept covered and refrigerated up to 2 hours. Whip the cream briefly to re-combine if it separates.

ANNE SAYS
"If the cream is to be piped, take care not to overwhip it because the cream will be worked further when it is forced through the piping bag."

1 Pour cream into a chilled bowl. Set over iced water if kitchen is hot.

2 Whip the cream with a whisk or electric mixer until it forms soft peaks.

3 Add sugar and flavouring and whip until the cream forms soft peaks again and just holds its shape.

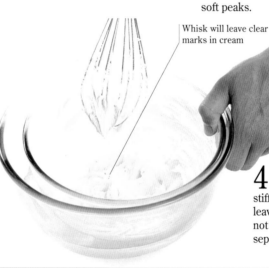

Whisk will leave clear marks in cream

4 Continue whipping until the cream forms stiff peaks and the whisk leaves clear marks. Do not overwhip or it will separate.

3 ASSEMBLE THE SHORTCAKES

1 Cut each of the cooled shortcakes in half horizontally with the serrated knife.

! TAKE CARE !
The shortcakes are quite crumbly.

2 Spoon the sliced strawberries with a little of their liquid onto the bottom halves of the shortcakes. Pile the Chantilly cream on the strawberries and top each one with its lid.

3 Top each shortcake with 2 of the strawberry fans.

4 Spoon the strawberry coulis on each plate and set a shortcake in the centre.

Place strawberry shortcake on coulis just before serving

Strawberry fans make pretty garnish for top of shortcake

Strawberry coulis, here flavoured with kirsch, beautifully complements shortcake

V A R I A T I O N

LEMON SHORTCAKES WITH BLUEBERRIES

This is only one of many possible variations of Strawberry Shortcakes. The lemon accents the blueberry filling. Choose blueberries that are firm and plump, discarding any that are very soft.

1 Make the shortcakes as directed, adding the grated zest and juice of 1 medium lemon with the unsalted butter.
2 Pick over 500 g (1 lb) blueberries; they do not need to be sprinkled with sugar.
3 Assemble the shortcakes, piling the blueberries on top of the Chantilly cream, and decorate each with a flower or herb sprig.

PAVLOVA WITH TROPICAL FRUIT

 SERVES 6-8   WORK TIME 25-30 MINUTES   BAKING TIME 2-2½ HOURS

EQUIPMENT

2 palette knives

chef's knife

sieve

pencil

whisk*

small knife

bowls

large metal spoon

wooden spoon

rubber spatula

piping bag and star nozzle

20 cm (8 inch) round cake tin

parchment paper

wire rack

baking sheet

chopping board

* electric mixer can also be used

INGREDIENTS

mangoes

pineapple

caster sugar

kiwi fruit

egg whites

kirsch

distilled malt vinegar

cornflour

double cream

vanilla essence

A giant meringue puff, with a crisp outside and soft, chewy interior, filled with whipped cream and fruit. This luscious dessert was created for famous ballerina Anna Pavlova, who was a frequent visitor to Australia and New Zealand, where the dessert originated.

GETTING AHEAD

The meringue can be baked and kept up to 1 week in an airtight container. It can also be frozen. Make the Pavlova filling and Chantilly cream not more than 2 hours ahead, assembling the Pavlova just before serving.

metric	SHOPPING LIST	imperial
5	medium kiwi fruit	5
1	pineapple, weighing about 750 g (1½ lb)	1
3	mangoes, total weight about 1 kg (2 lb)	3
45 g	caster sugar	1½ oz
30 ml	kirsch	2 tbsp
	For the meringue	
6	egg whites	6
350 g	caster sugar	12 oz
15 ml	cornflour	1 tbsp
5 ml	distilled malt vinegar	1 tsp
	For the Chantilly cream	
375 ml	double cream	12 fl oz
45-60 g	caster or icing sugar	1½-2 oz
5 ml	vanilla essence	1 tsp

ORDER OF WORK

1 MAKE THE MERINGUE

2 PREPARE THE PAVLOVA FILLING

3 ASSEMBLE THE PAVLOVA

1 MAKE THE MERINGUE

1 Line the baking sheet
with parchment paper.
Using the upturned cake tin as a
guide, draw a circle on the paper.
Heat the oven to 120°C (250°F, Gas ½).

2 Whisk the egg whites until stiff
(see box, right). Sprinkle in
75 g (2½ oz) of the sugar and continue
whisking until glossy to make a light
meringue, about 20 seconds. Sift the
cornflour and remaining sugar over the
egg whites and add the vinegar.

3 Fold the mixture together: cut
down into the centre of the bowl
with the rubber spatula, scoop under
the contents, and turn them over in a
rolling motion. At the same time, with
your other hand, turn the bowl anti-
clockwise. Continue folding until
thoroughly mixed.

HOW TO WHISK EGG WHITES UNTIL STIFF

*Egg whites should be whisked until
stiff but not dry. In order for them
to whisk properly, the whites, bowl,
and whisk must be completely free
from any trace of water, grease,
or egg yolk. A copper bowl and a
large balloon whisk are the classic
French utensils for whisking egg
whites. A metal or glass bowl with
a balloon whisk or an electric
mixer can also be used.*

1 Begin whisking whites slowly.
When they become foamy and
white, increase the whisking speed.
If you like, add a small pinch of salt
or cream of tartar to help achieve
maximum volume.

! TAKE CARE !
*Do not slow down the whisking
once the whites form soft peaks or
they may "turn", becoming grainy.*

2 The whites are whisked
enough if they form a stiff
peak when the whisk is lifted,
gathering in the whisk wires and
sticking without falling. The
whites should be used at once or
they will separate.

! TAKE CARE !
*Do not overbeat the egg whites;
the correct texture cannot be
reconstituted.*

4 Pile the meringue in the centre of the circle drawn on the paper, making sure the meringue keeps within the line.

5 With the back of the large metal spoon, spread out the meringue to an even round, making a deep hollow in the centre. Bake the meringue in the heated oven until firm and very lightly coloured, 2-2½ hours.

Handle carefully with palette knives to ensure Pavlova remains intact

! TAKE CARE !
If the meringue starts to brown during cooking, lower the heat and cover it loosely with foil.

6 Let the Pavlova cool to lukewarm, then lift it off the baking sheet with 2 large palette knives and set it on the wire rack to cool completely. When cold, peel off the paper.

ANNE SAYS
"The exterior of the baked meringue will become crisp as it cools, while the interior stays moist and chewy."

PREPARE THE PAVLOVA FILLING

1 With the small knife, trim the ends of the kiwi fruit. Set the fruit upright and trim off the skin in strips, working from top to bottom.

Follow curve of fruit when removing skin

2 Cut the kiwi fruit crosswise into neat slices.

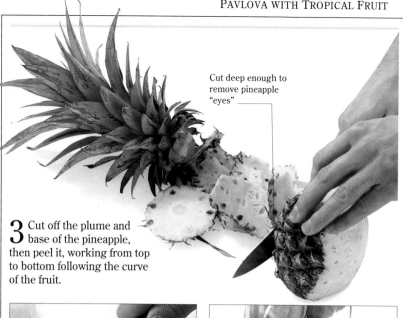

Cut deep enough to
remove pineapple
"eyes"

3 Cut off the plume and
base of the pineapple,
then peel it, working from top
to bottom following the curve
of the fruit.

HOW TO PEEL, STONE, AND CUBE MANGO

*Removing the flat, central stone,
and cubing mango flesh neatly,
is easy if you use this method.*

1 Cut each mango into 2 pieces
lengthwise, slightly off-centre
to just miss the stone. Cut the flesh
away from the other side of the
stone. Discard the stone.

2 Slash one piece in a lattice,
cutting through the flesh but
not the skin. Repeat with the other
piece of the mango.

3 Holding the mango flesh
upwards, push the centre of
the skin with your thumbs to turn
it inside out, opening the cuts of
flesh to reveal cubes. Cut the
cubes away from the skin.

4 Cut the pineapple lengthwise in
half, then into quarters. Cut out
the core from each quarter. Cut the
quarters lengthwise into strips, then
crosswise into neat chunks.

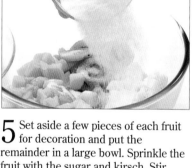

5 Set aside a few pieces of each fruit
for decoration and put the
remainder in a large bowl. Sprinkle the
fruit with the sugar and kirsch. Stir
gently with the wooden spoon to
distribute evenly, taking care not to
break up any of the fruit pieces.

6 Make the Chantilly
cream: pour the cream
into a chilled bowl and whip
until soft peaks form. Add the
sugar and vanilla essence and
continue whipping until stiff
peaks form.

Add sugar and
vanilla together,
once cream has
formed soft
peaks

HOW TO FILL A PIPING BAG AND PIPE ROSETTES

A large star piping nozzle is used to pipe decorations of Chantilly cream and meringue with a professional finish.

1 Drop the nozzle into the piping bag and twist, tucking the bag into the nozzle. This will prevent any cream from leaking out at the bottom.

2 Fold the top of the bag over your hand to form a collar and add the cream or meringue, using a rubber spatula or pastry scraper and scraping it against the bag.

3 When the bag is full, twist the top until there is no air left in it. When piping, hold the twisted top of the bag between your thumb and forefinger and squeeze the bag gently to press out the cream. Do not squeeze the bag with your other hand, but simply use it to help guide the nozzle as you pipe.

For a flower rosette: hold the nozzle upright and not quite touching the surface to be decorated. Press the bag until the flower rosette is the size wanted, then stop pressing as you lift the nozzle upwards.

For a swirled rosette: hold the nozzle near the surface to be decorated. Pressing evenly, move the nozzle in a tight circle to form the rosette. Stop pressing before lifting the nozzle. To make a ring or border of swirled rosettes, start and stop each rosette in the same place and make them all clockwise or anticlockwise.

For a rope: with the tip of the nozzle on the surface to be decorated, pipe a swirl in a clockwise movement. Do not lift the nozzle, but repeat, making another swirl next to the first. Continue until the rope is completed.

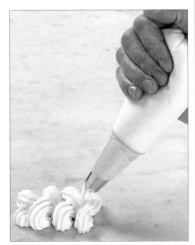

For a rope of double shells: hold the nozzle at a slight angle, touching the surface to be decorated. To pipe a shell, move the nozzle forwards and then up and down, back towards you, pressing evenly. Do not lift the nozzle, but continue piping shells, first in one direction, then in another, until the rope is completed.

3 ASSEMBLE THE PAVLOVA

1 Put the cooled Pavlova on a serving plate and spoon in half of the Chantilly cream.

2 Arrange the mixed fruit over the Chantilly cream.

3 Put the remaining Chantilly cream into the piping bag and pipe flower rosettes (see box, page 20) over the fruit. Arrange the reserved fruit on top and serve immediately.

Tropical fruit is framed by circle of meringue

PAVLOVA WITH MIXED BERRIES

Berries and meringue are a classic pair. Any variety of fresh berries can be used in place of the tropical fruit, but be sure that the berries are ripe and full of flavour.

1 Prepare the meringue as directed and put it into a large piping bag fitted with a large star nozzle.
2 Starting in the centre, pipe a disk of meringue inside the circle drawn on the parchment paper. Pipe a rope of double shells around the edge of the disk (see box, page 20) to form a "wall". Bake as directed.
3 Pick over 500 g (1 lb) mixed berries (strawberries, raspberries, blueberries, blackberries), washing them only if they are dirty. Hull the strawberries. Set aside a few of each for decoration and put the rest in a large bowl. Sprinkle with 45 ml (3 tbsp) sugar and 30 ml (2 tbsp) kirsch.
4 Fill the Pavlova with the fruit and Chantilly cream as directed, piping the reserved cream on top of the fruit, in ropes radiating from the centre (see box, page 20).

SUMMER FRUIT SALAD

🍽 SERVES 8-10   🥣 WORK TIME 40-45 MINUTES*

EQUIPMENT

bowls

cherry stoner

small saucepan

small knife

chef's knife

metal spoon

melon baller

slotted spoon

wooden spoon

cling film

chopping board

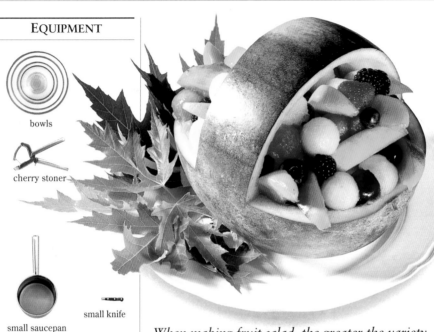

When making fruit salad, the greater the variety of fruit the better, so add to the suggestions here or substitute whatever fruit is in season. If you have any leftover fruit salad, you can serve it the next day, topped with scoops of vanilla ice cream.

GETTING AHEAD

The fruit salad can be kept in the watermelon basket, covered, in the refrigerator 6-8 hours.

* plus 4 hours soaking time

metric	SHOPPING LIST	imperial
1	medium watermelon	1
175 g	black cherries	6 oz
250 g	mixed berries, such as strawberries, raspberries, blueberries, blackberries	8 oz
1	honeydew or cantaloupe melon, weighing about 625 g (1¼ lb)	1
2	large peaches	2
2	large nectarines	2
	For soaking	
60 g	caster sugar	2 oz
125 ml	freshly squeezed orange juice	4 fl oz
30-45 ml	Grand Marnier (optional)	2-3 tbsp

INGREDIENTS

watermelon

honeydew melon

mixed berries

black cherries

nectarines

Grand Marnier (optional)

peaches

freshly squeezed orange juice

caster sugar

ANNE SAYS

"When choosing watermelon, shake to test if seeds are loose and ripe. Other types of melon should smell fragrant, and feel tender when pressed where the flower has fallen."

ORDER OF WORK

1 PREPARE THE WATERMELON BASKET

2 PREPARE THE FRUIT SALAD

3 SOAK AND FINISH THE FRUIT SALAD

1 PREPARE THE WATERMELON BASKET

1 With the chef's knife, cut a thin slice from one side of the watermelon so that it sits steady on the work surface.

2 Cut vertically into the melon about 2.5 cm (1 inch) from the centre of its length, cutting to the middle of the melon. Turn the melon and repeat on the other side, so that you have a 5 cm (2 inch) wide band in the centre.

4 With the small knife, cut around the flesh under the "handle" in a half-moon shape and remove it.

3 From the end of the melon, cut horizontally towards the centre, removing the wedge of melon. Repeat on the other side.

5 Using the melon baller, cut balls from the watermelon flesh in the bottom of the basket. Remove the seeds and put the balls in a large bowl.

Shape neat balls with special cutter

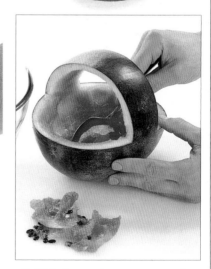

Flick out seeds with tip of small knife

6 With the metal spoon, remove the remaining bits of flesh from the melon cavity. Chill the melon basket until serving.

! TAKE CARE !
Do not pierce the bottom of the melon basket or the fruit juice will leak.

2 PREPARE THE FRUIT SALAD

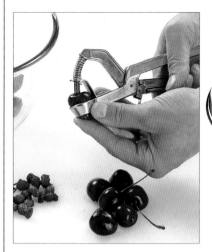

1 Stone the cherries and add them to the bowl with the watermelon balls.

ANNE SAYS
"If you do not have a cherry stoner, you can scoop out the stones with the tip of a vegetable peeler."

3 Halve the honeydew or cantaloupe melon; scoop out and discard the seeds. With the melon baller, cut balls from the flesh, and add them to the fruit in the bowl.

Different fruit will make pretty filling

2 Pick over the berries, washing them only if they are dirty. Hull strawberries; if they are large, halve or quarter them. Add the berries to the watermelon and cherries.

Small knife cuts hulls neatly from strawberries

Scrape out any fibres from centre of melon along with seeds

4 Immerse the peaches in boiling water in the saucepan, leave 10 seconds, then transfer with the slotted spoon to a bowl of cold water. Cut each peach in half, remove the stone, and peel off the skin. Cut each half into 6 wedges and add to the bowl. Cut each nectarine in half, remove the stone and cut each half into 6 wedges.

3 SOAK AND FINISH THE FRUIT SALAD

1 Sprinkle the sugar over the fruit, then pour over the orange juice, and Grand Marnier, if using. Stir gently with the wooden spoon. Cover the bowl with cling film and leave to soak in the refrigerator 4 hours, stirring occasionally.

! TAKE CARE !
Stir gently so you do not break up the fruit pieces.

2 Spoon the fruit salad and juice into the watermelon basket. Serve chilled.

VARIATION

ALTERNATIVE MELON CONTAINERS

Any melon can be shaped as a basket or bowl for fruit salads. Here are three alternatives to the watermelon basket.

Melon casket with scalloped edge
1 Make a horizontal cut halfway round the top quarter of the melon. Turn uncut side towards you; cut 3 or 4 deep scallops.
2 Pull off the top of the melon; scoop out and discard the seeds and fibres.
3 Use a melon baller to scoop out balls of flesh, then scrape out the remaining flesh so that the insides of the melon top and the base are smooth.
4 Make a cut in the flat top edge of the melon base and insert the flat edge of the melon top into the groove so that it rests over the base at an angle.
5 Mix the melon balls with other melon balls; pile them in the casket.

Melon bowl with wolves' teeth edge
1 Force the tip of a chef's knife down through the middle of the melon at a 45° angle, making a 1 cm (¹⁄₂ inch) slit.
2 Remove the knife and reinsert it at a 45° angle to meet the tip of the first incision. Continue in this fashion around the melon until the wolves' teeth meet at the first cut.
3 Separate the melon halves, and scoop out and discard the seeds and fibres. Fill with fruit.

Simple melon bowl
1 Choose small melons and cut each one in half. Scoop out and discard the seeds and fibres, then use a melon baller to scoop out balls of flesh.
2 With a metal spoon, scrape out the remaining flesh so that the inside of each melon half is smooth.
3 Mix the melon balls with other fruit and melon balls, and spoon into the melon bowls.

VARIATION
EXOTIC FRUIT SALAD

With modern transportation, exotic fruit are no longer restricted to their country of origin and we can enjoy different kinds of fruit from around the world all year long. They do not keep well, so buy fully ripe fruit and keep them as short a time as possible to use in this variation of Summer Fruit Salad.

1 Peel 1 pineapple (weighing about 750 g/1½ lb), then cut it lengthwise in half and remove the core. Slice each half crosswise.

2 Cut the flesh into chunks and put them in a large bowl.

3 Cut 2 papayas (total weight about 500 g/1 lb) lengthwise in half. Scoop out and discard the dark seeds.

4 Cut the papayas into quarters. Holding the papaya quarters with the skin side towards you, remove the skin from each quarter with a small knife.

5 With a chef's knife, cut the papaya flesh into chunks the same size as the pineapple chunks and add to the bowl.

6 Trim the ends of 3 kiwi fruit. Set the fruit upright on the work surface and trim off the skin in strips, working from top to bottom following the curve of the kiwi fruit. Cut the fruit lengthwise into quarters, then slice. Add to the bowl.

7 Cut 2 large mangoes lengthwise into 2 pieces, slightly off-centre so the knife just misses the stone. Cut the flesh away from the stone. Repeat on the other side. Discard the stone. Slash the mango flesh in a lattice, not cutting through the peel, then carefully push each half inside out, opening the cuts to reveal cubes. Cut the cubes of flesh away from the skin and add them to the bowl.

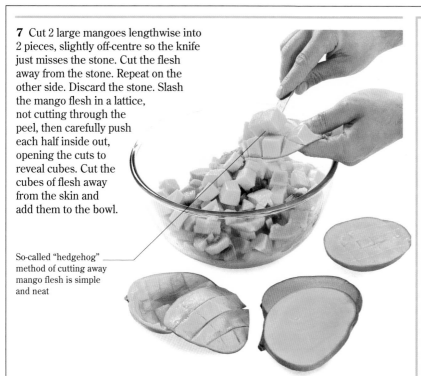

So-called "hedgehog" method of cutting away mango flesh is simple and neat

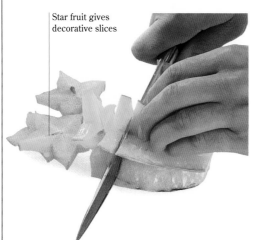

Star fruit gives decorative slices

8 Trim and discard the ends from 2 star fruit. Cut the fruit into 1 cm (½ inch) thick slices and add them to the bowl. Shell 250 g (8 oz) fresh lychees with a small knife, remove the stalk end, and peel away the skin. Slit the lychee flesh on one side and remove the stone from the centre. Alternatively, drain a 250 g (8 oz) can of lychees. Add to the bowl.

9 Remove the seeds from 1 pomegranate (see box, right) and add to the bowl. Soak the fruit salad as directed in the main recipe, replacing the orange juice with white wine and the Grand Marnier with rum.

HOW TO REMOVE POMEGRANATE SEEDS

Take care when cutting into the pomegranate because if the seeds puncture the juice will leak out.

1 Using the point of a small knife, cut around the blossom end of the fruit to remove it.

2 With the tip of the knife, score the skin in quarters, taking care not to puncture any of the juicy seeds inside.

3 Working over a bowl, break the fruit in half using your hands, following the score lines. Break each half into quarters.

4 Peel the hard skin back from each quarter, releasing the seeds into the bowl. Discard any pieces of membrane.

APRICOT MOUSSE

EQUIPMENT

vegetable peeler

small knife

food processor** lemon squeezer

whisk***

sieve   wooden spoon

slotted spoon

parchment paper   small heatproof plate

1.5 litre (2¹/₂ pint) ring mould   piping bag and star nozzle

saucepans

bowls

rubber spatula

** blender can also be used
*** electric mixer can also be used

For this delicate mousse choose fine, fresh apricots with a deep gold colour, intense perfume, and soft, velvety skin.

GETTING AHEAD

The mousse can be prepared and chilled up to 24 hours ahead. Unmould and decorate not more than 1 hour before serving.

* plus at least 2 hours chilling time

INGREDIENTS

lemon

egg yolks

caster sugar

powdered gelatine

apricots

kirsch

eggs

double cream

vanilla essence

metric	SHOPPING LIST	imperial
	For poaching the apricots	
1	lemon	1
1 litre	water	1²/₃ pints
200 g	caster sugar	6¹/₂ oz
	For the apricot mousse	
1 kg	apricots	2 lb
250 ml	double cream	8 fl oz
15 g	powdered gelatine	¹/₂ oz
2	eggs	2
2	egg yolks	2
150 g	caster sugar	5 oz
30 ml	kirsch	2 tbsp
	For the Chantilly cream	
125 ml	double cream	4 fl oz
15-30 ml	caster sugar	1-2 tbsp
2.5 ml	vanilla essence	¹/₂ tsp

ORDER OF WORK

1 POACH THE APRICOTS

2 PREPARE THE APRICOT MOUSSE

3 UNMOULD AND DECORATE THE MOUSSE WITH CHANTILLY CREAM AND APRICOTS

1 POACH THE APRICOTS

Use indentation on apricot as guide for cutting

1 With the vegetable peeler, pare the zest from the lemon. Squeeze the juice from the lemon.

2 Halve and stone the apricots. Set aside 2 apricot halves for decoration.

3 Put the water, lemon zest, and lemon juice in a medium saucepan and add the sugar. Heat until the sugar has dissolved, then bring to a boil and cook 2 minutes.

Pour out hot mixture carefully

Hold sieve over bowl to collect poaching liquid

4 Add the apricots to the syrup. Cover them with a round of parchment paper and set the heatproof plate on top to weigh them down. Poach until very tender, 10-15 minutes.

5 Drain the apricots, reserving 125 ml (4 fl oz) of the poaching liquid.

2 PREPARE THE APRICOT MOUSSE

1 Purée the apricots in the food processor; there should be about 750 ml (1¼ pints) of purée. Pour the cream into a chilled bowl and whip until it forms soft peaks, then chill it. Soften the gelatine in the reserved liquid (see box, right).

3 Melt the softened gelatine (see box, right) and whisk it into the tepid apricot mixture. Continue whisking until cool.

! TAKE CARE !
The mixture must be warm when the gelatine is added or the gelatine may set instantly and form lumps.

4 Set the bowl over iced water and stir the mixture until it begins to thicken. Working quickly, fold in the whipped cream and kirsch. Cut down into the centre of the bowl, scoop under the contents and turn mixture over with a rolling motion.

2 In the medium saucepan, whisk together the eggs, egg yolks, sugar, and apricot purée until well blended. Cook the mixture, stirring constantly, just until it boils. Pour the mixture into a large bowl and whisk thoroughly until it is light and cooled to tepid, 5-7 minutes.

5 Pour the mousse into the mould. Chill until the mousse is firmly set, at least 2 hours.

ANNE SAYS
"Gelatine tends to stiffen on chilling, so let the mousse stand at room temperature about 1 hour before serving if it has been made ahead."

HOW TO USE POWDERED GELATINE

Gelatine must be softened and melted carefully because it easily cooks into strings or forms lumps when it is added to other mixtures.

1 To soften the gelatine: pour the water, or other liquid called for in the recipe, into a small saucepan and sprinkle the gelatine evenly on top of the liquid.

2 Let soak about 5 minutes; the gelatine will swell to a spongy consistency.

3 To melt the gelatine: warm the saucepan over very low heat, or set it in a large bowl of hot water. Heat gently without stirring, shaking the pan occasionally. Stir the warm melted gelatine into a tepid mixture until evenly distributed.

! TAKE CARE !
Do not stir the gelatine during melting, or it may form lumps.

3 UNMOULD AND DECORATE THE MOUSSE WITH CHANTILLY CREAM AND APRICOTS

1 Run the small knife around the edge of the mould, then dip the base of the mould in a bowl of warm water for a few seconds to loosen the mousse. Dry the mould base, set a serving plate on top of the mould, and invert the mousse onto the plate.

ANNE SAYS
"If the mousse sticks, coax the sides away with your fingers."

2 To make the Chantilly cream, pour the cream into a chilled bowl and whip until soft peaks form when the whisk is lifted. Add the sugar and vanilla essence and continue whipping until stiff peaks form. Take care not to overbeat because the cream will be worked further when forced through the piping bag. If it is too stiff, the cream will separate.

3 Fill the piping bag with the Chantilly cream. Decorate the base and top of the mousse with small stars, and the centre with a circle of piping. Slice the reserved apricot halves and complete the decoration.

STRAWBERRY MOUSSE WITH FRESH PLUM SAUCE

1 Substitute 750 g (1½ lb) strawberries for the apricots. Hull the strawberries, washing them only if they are dirty. Set aside 8 small strawberries with hulls for decoration and purée the rest in a food processor or blender.

2 Make the mousse as directed, softening the gelatine in 125 ml (4 fl oz) water. Fill eight 175 ml (6 fl oz) ramekins or moulds.

3 While the mousse is chilling, prepare a plum sauce: halve and stone 250 g (8 oz) purple plums. Poach them as for apricots. Drain the plums, reserving the poaching liquid, and purée in the food processor or blender.

4 Add enough of the reserved poaching liquid to the puréed plums to make a pourable sauce.

5 Unmould each mousse onto an individual plate. Omit the Chantilly cream rosettes and top each mousse with a strawberry. Spoon some of the plum sauce around each mousse and serve the rest separately.

Chantilly cream is piped into stars to decorate mousse

COLD LEMON SOUFFLE

🍽 SERVES 8 ⊌ WORK TIME 35-40 MINUTES ❄ CHILLING TIME 2-3 HOURS

EQUIPMENT

souffle dish

lemon squeezer

aluminium foil

sieve

teaspoon

electric mixer

vegetable peeler

grater

saucepans

small knife

piping bag and medium star nozzle

rubber spatula

kitchen scissors

fork

plate

whisk

bowls

chopping board

palette knife

tape

One of the all-time best endings to a grand dinner, lemon soufflé is cool, light, and fluffy, with just the right balance of tart and sweet. Choose lemons with bright, even colour, and smooth rather than pitted skin.

GETTING AHEAD

The soufflé can be made, and the lemon zest candied, 1 day ahead and kept, covered, in the refrigerator. The soufflé can be decorated with Chantilly cream and candied zest, then refrigerated up to 4 hours. Remove the collar just before serving.

INGREDIENTS

lemons

egg whites

eggs

caster sugar

vanilla essence

powdered gelatine

double cream

ANNE SAYS

"Gelatine mixtures tend to stiffen on chilling, so if you prepare the soufflé ahead, let it stand at room temperature about 1 hour before serving."

ORDER OF WORK

1 PREPARE THE SOUFFLE DISH

2 MAKE THE LEMON SOUFFLE BASE

3 FINISH AND CHILL THE SOUFFLE

4 DECORATE THE SOUFFLE

metric	SHOPPING LIST	imperial
200 ml	water	6½ fl oz
10 g	powdered gelatine	⅓ oz
4	large lemons	4
4	eggs	4
250 g	caster sugar	8 oz
250 ml	double cream	8 fl oz
2	egg whites	2
	For the candied zest	
30 ml	caster sugar	2 tbsp
30 ml	water	2 tbsp
	For the Chantilly cream	
125 ml	double cream	4 fl oz
15-30 ml	caster sugar	1-2 tbsp
2.5 ml	vanilla essence	½ tsp

1 PREPARE THE SOUFFLE DISH

1 Cut a piece of foil 5 cm (2 inches) longer than the circumference of a 1 litre (1¾ pint) soufflé dish. Fold the foil lengthwise in half.

Fold the foil in half to increase strength

2 Wrap the foil around the dish. It should stand well above the rim. Secure the foil with tape.

ANNE SAYS
"So the soufflé appears to have 'risen', the foil should reach above the rim."

2 MAKE THE LEMON SOUFFLE BASE

Sprinkle gelatine evenly over water in pan

1 Put 75 ml (2½ fl oz) of the water in a small saucepan, sprinkle the gelatine on top, and set aside to soften until spongy, about 5 minutes.

2 Grate the zest from 3 of the lemons. Pare strips of zest from the remaining lemon and reserve it to candy. Squeeze the juice from all 4 lemons – there should be 150 ml (5 fl oz).

3 Separate the whole eggs. In a medium saucepan, mix together the egg yolks, grated lemon zest, and lemon juice, and two-thirds of the sugar until blended.

4 Cook, stirring, just until mixture boils. Pour into a large bowl and beat with the electric mixer until light and thick enough to leave a ribbon trail when the whisk is lifted, 5-7 minutes.

5 Warm the gelatine over low heat, shaking the pan, until the gelatine is melted and pourable, 1-2 minutes; do not stir. Whisk into the lemon mixture and continue whisking until cool.

3 FINISH AND CHILL THE SOUFFLE

1 Pour the cream into a chilled bowl and whip until soft peaks form; chill the cream.

2 Heat the remaining sugar with the remaining water in a small saucepan until dissolved. Boil without stirring until the syrup reaches the hard ball stage. To test, take the pan from the heat, dip a teaspoon in the hot syrup, remove, and let cool a few seconds. Take a little syrup between your finger and thumb. It should form a firm, pliable ball.

ANNE SAYS
"*If you have a sugar thermometer, you can use it to test the syrup; it should register 120°C (248°F).*"

! TAKE CARE !
Dip your fingers in cold water before testing the syrup.

3 While the syrup is boiling, put the 6 egg whites in a bowl and whisk. Begin whisking slowly, but increase speed when they become foamy and white. Continue whisking until stiff peaks form when the whisk is lifted.

Pour syrup in thin, steady stream

4 Gradually pour the hot sugar syrup into the egg whites, whisking constantly.

Electric mixer takes over from balloon whisk

5 Continue whisking until the meringue is cool and stiff, about 5 minutes.

6 Set the bowl of lemon mixture in a larger bowl of iced water and stir the mixture gently until it starts to thicken. Remove the bowl from the ice bath.

Iced water helps mixture to thicken

Mixture will form mound when dropped from spatula

7 Fold in the whipped cream, then fold in the meringue in 2 batches (see box, right).

! TAKE CARE !
Work quickly because the mixture sets fast.

Scrape mixture from bowl with rubber spatula

Pour mixture into centre of dish

8 Pour the soufflé mixture into the prepared soufflé dish – it should come at least 5 cm (2 inches) above the rim of the dish but below the edge of the foil collar. Chill the soufflé until firmly set, at least 2 hours.

HOW TO CUT AND FOLD MIXTURES TOGETHER

Two mixtures can be folded together most easily if their consistency is similar. If one ingredient is much lighter or more liquid than the other, such as stiffly whisked egg whites and fruit purée, first thoroughly stir a little of the lighter mixture into the heavier one to soften it.

1 Spoon one mixture over the other as directed in the recipe. With a rubber spatula, or a wooden or metal spoon, cut down into the centre of the bowl.

2 Scoop under the contents and turn them over in a rolling motion. At the same time, with your other hand, turn the bowl anticlockwise. Continue folding gently until the mixtures are thoroughly combined.

ANNE SAYS
"This should be a synchronized movement: cut and scoop with the spatula in one hand, turn the bowl with the other. In this way, the spatula reaches the maximum volume of mixture in one movement, so that it is folded quickly and loses a minimum of air."

HOW TO CUT AND CANDY LEMON ZEST

Candied zest adds texture and flavour to creamy desserts.

1 Cut pared zest of lemon into very fine strips.

2 Bring a small pan of water to a boil, add the zest strips and simmer 2 minutes, then drain.

3 In the same pan, gently heat the sugar with the measured water until dissolved. Add the zest and simmer until all the water has evaporated, 8-10 minutes.

4 Remove the zest with a fork and set aside to cool.

4 DECORATE THE SOUFFLE

1 Candy the reserved lemon zest (see box, left). To make the Chantilly cream, pour the cream into a chilled bowl and whip until soft peaks form. Add the sugar and vanilla essence and continue whipping until the cream forms stiff peaks and the whisk leaves clear marks in the cream.

Kitchen scissors cut foil neatly

2 With the kitchen scissors, carefully trim the foil collar level with the top of the soufflé mixture.

Smooth cream with palette knife

3 Spread about one-third of the Chantilly cream over the top of the soufflé.

4 With the tines of the fork, mark a lattice design in the cream.

5 Fill the piping bag with the remaining Chantilly cream and pipe a scroll border around the edge of the soufflé.

6 Top the piped cream with the candied lemon zest.

Candied lemon zest
forms a brightly coloured
decoration

Ease foil away
gently, using
small knife

†❶† TO SERVE
Carefully remove the foil collar from
the soufflé. Place the soufflé dish
on a serving plate.

Soufflé looks as
though it has risen
above the dish

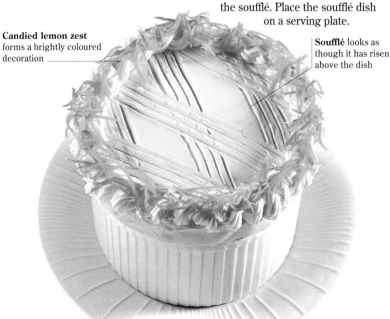

V A R I A T I O N
INDIVIDUAL COLD LIME SOUFFLÉS

Lime is another favourite citrus fruit that adapts well to a cold soufflé. Look for limes that are plump, with even colour and unblemished skin.

1 Instead of using a large soufflé dish, prepare eight 125 ml (4 fl oz) ramekins with foil collars, as directed.
2 Replace the lemons with 6 limes. Grate the zest from 4 of the limes and squeeze the juice from all of them.
3 Continue with the soufflé, but omit the candied zest.
4 Put 24 unsalted pistachio nuts in a bowl, cover them generously with boiling water, and let soak 5 minutes, then drain them. Rub off the skins with your fingers.
5 Decorate each soufflé with rosettes of Chantilly cream and the pistachio nuts.

PEAR AND REDCURRANT COMPOTE

 SERVES 4   WORK TIME 15-20 MINUTES* COOKING TIME ABOUT 45 MINUTES

EQUIPMENT

whisk**

lemon squeezer

fork

slotted spoon

metal spoon

small knife

vegetable peeler

parchment paper

heatproof plate

bowls

small deep saucepan   baking sheet

**electric mixer can also be used

Here pears and redcurrants are
flavoured with vanilla and crème de cassis, topped
with almonds, and served with cassis-spiked
Chantilly cream. For poaching, choose fruit that
is juicy and ripe, yet firm; very ripe fruit tends to
break up when poached. If you cannot find
crème de cassis, substitute blackcurrant syrup.

GETTING AHEAD
The pears and redcurrants can be poached up to 3 days
ahead and kept, covered in their poaching liquid, in the
refrigerator. Make the cassis Chantilly cream not more than
2 hours before serving.

plus chilling time

metric	SHOPPING LIST	imperial
4	firm pears, total weight about 750 g (1½ lb)	4
2	lemons	2
125 g	redcurrants	4 oz
100 g	caster sugar	3½ oz
500 ml	water	16 fl oz
30 ml	crème de cassis (blackcurrant liqueur)	2 tbsp
1	vanilla pod or 5 ml (1 tsp) vanilla essence	1
45 g	flaked almonds	1½ oz
For the cassis Chantilly cream		
250 ml	double cream	8 fl oz
15-30 ml	icing sugar	1-2 tbsp
15-30 ml	crème de cassis (blackcurrant liqueur)	1-2 tbsp

INGREDIENTS

pears

redcurrants

vanilla pod

double cream

crème de cassis

caster sugar

icing sugar***

flaked almonds

lemons

***caster sugar can also be used

ORDER OF WORK

1 PREPARE THE PEARS AND REDCURRANTS

2 POACH THE PEARS AND REDCURRANTS

3 TOAST THE ALMONDS; MAKE CHANTILLY CREAM

1 PREPARE THE PEARS AND REDCURRANTS

Fork tines exert light, deft pressure

1 Peel the pears, leaving the stalks intact. Cut one of the lemons in half and rub lemon juice all over the pears to prevent discoloration.

2 Working from the bottom, scoop out the pips and fibrous core from each pear with the vegetable peeler.

! TAKE CARE !
Do not break pears open when coring.

3 Pick over the redcurrants and pull them from the stalks with the tines of the fork.

2 POACH THE PEARS AND REDCURRANTS

Choose deep saucepan so fruit will be immersed in syrup

1 Pare the zest from the second lemon and squeeze the juice from it. Combine the lemon zest and juice, sugar, water, and split-open vanilla pod, if using, in the saucepan and heat until the sugar has dissolved.

2 Bring the poaching liquid to a boil, remove the saucepan from the heat, and add the whole pears.

ANNE SAYS
"The fruit should be completely covered by syrup, so if necessary, add more water to cover."

Test pears are tender with tip of small sharp knife

3 Cover the fruit with a round of parchment paper and set the heatproof plate on top to weigh them down. Simmer gently over low heat until the pears are almost tender, about 15-25 minutes depending on ripeness.

! TAKE CARE !
Do not let the liquid boil or the outside of the pears will disintegrate before the inside is cooked.

Be sure all stalks have been removed from redcurrants

4 Add the redcurrants to the pears, return the saucepan to the heat, and continue poaching until the pears are just tender, about 10 minutes longer. Remove from the heat and test the pears are tender with the tip of the small knife.

5 Let the fruit cool in the poaching liquid, then transfer both the pears and the redcurrants to a glass serving bowl using the slotted spoon.

6 Boil the poaching liquid until it forms a fairly thick syrup and is reduced by about half, 5-7 minutes. Stir in the crème de cassis with the vanilla essence, if using.

7 Let the syrup cool, then strain it and pour it over the pears and redcurrants. Cover the compote and chill while toasting the flaked almonds and making the cassis Chantilly cream.

3 TOAST THE ALMONDS; MAKE CHANTILLY CREAM

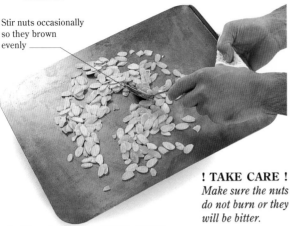

Stir nuts occasionally so they brown evenly

1 Heat the oven to 180°C (350°F, Gas 4). Toast the almonds until lightly browned, 8-10 minutes.

! TAKE CARE !
Make sure the nuts do not burn or they will be bitter.

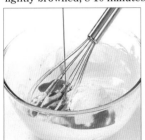

2 To make the Chantilly cream, pour the cream into a chilled bowl and whip until soft peaks form. Add the sugar and crème de cassis and continue whipping the cream until stiff peaks form.

🍽 **TO SERVE**

Sprinkle the toasted almonds over the fruit. Serve the cassis Chantilly cream in a separate bowl.

Toasted flaked almonds give crunchy texture contrast

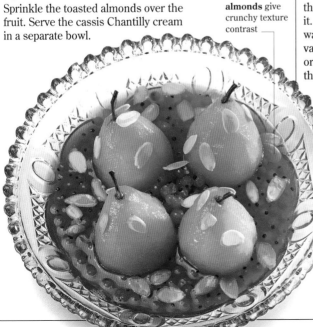

VARIATIONS

NECTARINE COMPOTE

Nectarines marry well with cardamom, while pistachios add a pretty colour contrast to this variation of pear compote.

1 Halve and stone 4 nectarines (total weight about 750 g/1½ lb); omit the pears and redcurrants.
2 Make the poaching syrup as directed, replacing the vanilla with 5 ml (1 tsp) lightly crushed cardamom pods.
3 Poach the nectarines until tender, about 5-7 minutes, then let cool in the poaching liquid before transferring to a bowl. Reduce the liquid to syrup as directed and strain.
4 To finish, omit the crème de cassis, toasted almonds, and cassis Chantilly cream. Put 30 g (1 oz) pistachio nuts in a bowl, cover generously with boiling water, and let soak 5 minutes, then drain. Rub off the skins with your fingers.
5 Sprinkle the pistachios over the nectarines and serve.

DRIED FRUIT COMPOTE

1 Pare the zest from 1 orange, then squeeze the juice from it. Bring 750 ml (1¼ pints) water to a boil with a vanilla pod, and the orange zest and juice, then add 125 g (4 oz) prunes and 125 g (4 oz) dried apricots. Poach the fruit 10 minutes.
2 Add 75 g (2½ oz) sultanas and continue to poach until all fruit is soft, about 10 minutes longer. Let cool, then remove the fruit.
3 Add the sugar and stir until dissolved, then bring to a boil and reduce the liquid to syrup as directed. Substitute rum for the crème de cassis.
4 To finish, omit the toasted almonds and cassis Chantilly cream. If you like, pare the zest from a second orange and candy it (see box, page 36). Use the candied zest to garnish the fruit.

MANGO SORBET

 MAKES 1.25 LITRES (2 PINTS) TO SERVE 6-8   WORK TIME 25-30 MINUTES   ❄ FREEZING TIME 4 HOURS

EQUIPMENT

lemon squeezer

small knife

chef's knife

rubber spatula

bowls

ice-cream maker

ice-cream scoop

small saucepan

vegetable peeler

teaspoon

sieve

food processor*   chopping board

*blender can also be used

INGREDIENTS

mangoes

orange juice

lemon juice

caster sugar

ANNE SAYS
"*If you would like to serve sorbet ovals instead of rounds, two tablespoons can be used to shape them. Dip the spoons in cold water. Use one to scoop a generous spoonful of sorbet, scraping off the excess against the bowl. Use the second spoon to shape an oval, then let the oval fall onto a chilled plate.*"

The key to good sorbet is smoothness; the ice crystals that form naturally during freezing must be forestalled. This is accomplished by stirring the mixture constantly, usually by machine. Simple and refreshing, this sorbet can be made with any number of fruit purées replacing the mango. As freezing diminishes flavour, be sure that the fruit are at their peak of ripeness. Lemon and orange juices add acid to balance sugar and heighten flavour. If you like, pour a splash of Champagne or vodka over the sorbet before serving.

— GETTING AHEAD —
Sorbet can be kept up to 1 week in the freezer. If frozen for more than 24 hours, let the sorbet soften in the refrigerator 30 minutes before serving.

metric	SHOPPING LIST	imperial
100 g	caster sugar, more if needed	3½ oz
125 ml	water	4 fl oz
3	mangoes, total weight 1.25-1.4 kg (2½-3 lb)	3
	juice of 1 lemon	
	juice of 1 orange	

ORDER OF WORK

1 **MAKE THE SUGAR SYRUP**

2 **MAKE THE SORBET MIXTURE AND FREEZE**

1 MAKE THE SUGAR SYRUP

1 Combine the sugar and water in the small saucepan.

Boil syrup until clear

Let syrup cool

2 Heat until the sugar has dissolved, then boil the syrup until it is clear, 2-3 minutes. Set aside to cool.

2 MAKE THE SORBET MIXTURE AND FREEZE

1 Peel the mangoes. Cut each mango lengthwise into 2 pieces, slightly off-centre to just miss the stone. Cut the flesh away from the other side of the stone.

2 Cut the remaining thin layer of flesh from the stone. Cut all the mango flesh into cubes.

Work in batches so purée will be smooth

3 Purée the mango flesh in batches, in the food processor.

4 With all the pureé in the food processor, and the blade turning, pour in the cooled syrup with the lemon and orange juices. The mixture will be quite thick. Taste it, adding more sugar if it is tart.

Amount of sugar for sorbet depends on tartness of fruit

5 Pour the sorbet mixture into the ice-cream maker and freeze until firm, following the manufacturer's directions. Meanwhile, chill the bowl for the sorbet in the freezer.

ANNE SAYS
"Chilling time varies greatly with the machine you use."

Sorbet mixture should not fill container completely

Crisp biscuits are perfect accompaniment

Mango sorbet is smooth and rich

TO SERVE
If necessary, transfer the sorbet to the refrigerator to soften slightly. Scoop the sorbet into chilled coupe glasses and serve immediately.

6 Transfer the sorbet to the chilled bowl. Cover it and freeze at least 4 hours to allow the flavour to mellow.

VARIATION
LEMON SORBET

*Hollowed-out lemons form
pretty individual serving dishes
for lemon sorbet.*

1 Hollow out 8 medium lemons to
make cups (see box, right). Press the
lemon flesh in a sieve set over a
measuring jug to extract as much juice
as possible.
2 Make the sugar syrup as directed,
using 500 ml (16 fl oz) water and 400 g
(13 oz) sugar; set aside to cool.
3 Grate the zest and squeeze the juice
from 3 lemons; add to the juice in the
measuring jug. If necessary, squeeze
the juice from 1-2 more lemons to
make 375 ml (12 fl oz).
4 Add the lemon juice and zest to the
cooled syrup and freeze as directed.
Put the lemon cups and lids on a tray
and freeze them, too.

5 After the sorbet has frozen in the
machine, spoon it directly into the
frozen lemon cups. Mound the tops
generously, add a lid, and freeze until
serving.
6 Just before serving, make a small slit
in each lid and insert the stem of a
lemon leaf, if you have one, or a bay
leaf. Put the lids on top of the sorbets.

VARIATION
MELON SORBET

*The flavour of ripe cantaloupe or honeydew
melon is heightened by the juices of lemon and
lime in this sorbet. Crisp biscuits are an ideal
accompaniment.*

1 Make the sugar syrup as directed, using
175 ml (6 fl oz) water and 400 g (13 oz) sugar;
set aside to cool.
2 Halve 1 large or 2 small melons (total weight
about 1.4 kg/3 lb); scoop out and discard the
seeds. Cut each half into 4 pieces and cut away
the rind.
3 Purée the melon flesh in the food processor or
blender and add the juice of 1 lemon and 1 lime
with the sugar syrup. Freeze as directed.
4 Just before serving, scoop balls of the sorbet
and pile them in chilled dessert glasses or dishes.

HOW TO MAKE LEMON OR ORANGE CUPS

*Citrus fruit are ideal for hollowing out and filling with
sorbet or fruit salad to serve in individual portions.*

1 Cut a lid from the top of each
fruit, and a slice from the base
so the fruit sits upright.

2 With the tip of a small knife, cut
into the fruit just inside the rind
to loosen the flesh.

3 Insert the knife horizontally into
the bottom of the fruit, making a
cut only 1 cm (1/2 inch) long. This
will loosen the flesh at the bottom.

4 Scoop out the flesh into a sieve
set over a measuring jug. Scrape
out any remaining flesh to leave a
clean hollow.

ORANGE CARAMEL CREAMS

Pudim de Laranja

 SERVES 4   WORK TIME 15-20 MINUTES*   BAKING TIME 20-25 MINUTES

EQUIPMENT

small knife

chef's knife

whisk

wooden spoon

lemon squeezer

plastic sieve

tea towel

small, heavy-based saucepan

4 medium ramekins (225 ml/7 fl oz)

bowls

roasting tin

chopping board

INGREDIENTS

oranges

eggs

caster sugar

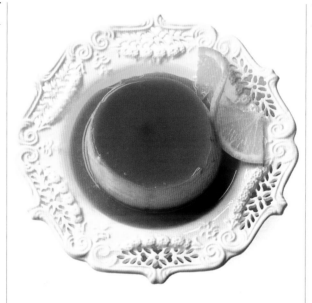

A version of crème caramel from Portugal to make your taste buds tingle, with a pretty orange colour, topped with a caramel sauce. The caramel sauce should be cooked to a deep golden brown for a rich flavour, which perfectly complements the fresh tang of oranges. For maximum juiciness and sweetness, choose oranges that feel heavy in your hand and have no blemishes on the skin.

GETTING AHEAD

The orange caramel creams can be prepared, baked up to 2 days ahead, and kept in the refrigerator. Unmould them just before serving; if left to stand the caramel will discolour.

* plus 2 hours chilling time

metric	SHOPPING LIST	imperial
	For the caramel	
75 ml	water	2$^{1}/_{2}$ fl oz
100 g	caster sugar	3$^{1}/_{2}$ oz
	For the orange cream	
4	large oranges	4
5	eggs	5
60 g	caster sugar	2 oz
	orange slices to garnish	

ANNE SAYS

"To maintain an even heat, plain custards and creams are cooked in a water bath. They should be taken from the heat as soon as they are cooked or even a little before, because they will continue to cook in retained heat."

ORDER OF WORK

1. MAKE THE CARAMEL

2. MAKE THE ORANGE CREAM MIXTURE

3. COOK AND UNMOULD THE ORANGE CARAMEL CREAMS

1 MAKE THE CARAMEL

1 Put the water in the saucepan, add the sugar, and cook over low heat until dissolved, stirring occasionally with the wooden spoon.

2 Boil the mixture, without stirring, until it starts to turn golden.

! TAKE CARE !
Do not stir the sugar during boiling, or it may crystallize.

3 Lower the heat and continue cooking, swirling the pan once or twice so the caramel syrup colours evenly.

Caramel should be richly coloured for best flavour

4 Cook until the syrup is deep golden in colour for best flavour. Do not overcook because caramel burns easily.

Tip and rotate ramekin to spread caramel evenly

5 Remove the pan from the heat and immediately plunge the base of the pan into a bowl of cold water to stop the cooking.

6 Pour the caramel into the ramekins, dividing it equally among them. Working quickly, tilt each ramekin so the bottom is coated with a thin, even layer. Set the dishes aside to cool.

! TAKE CARE !
The caramel is extremely hot.

2 MAKE THE ORANGE CREAM MIXTURE

1 Heat the oven to 180°C (350°F, Gas 4). Halve the oranges and squeeze the juice from them. There should be 500 ml (16 fl oz) of juice.

2 In a large bowl, whisk the eggs with the sugar until well mixed. Gently whisk in the orange juice.

3 Strain the mixture through the plastic sieve into a measuring jug so it is easy to pour.

3 COOK AND UNMOULD THE ORANGE CARAMEL CREAMS

Towel prevents water from bubbling up into creams

1 Carefully pour the orange cream mixture over the caramel in the ramekins.

2 Lay the tea towel on the bottom of the roasting tin and set the ramekins on the towel.

3 Pour hot water into the roasting tin to come more than halfway up the sides of the ramekins, to make a water bath. Bring the water to a boil on top of the stove, then transfer the tin to the heated oven.

Water bath protects delicate creams from direct heat

Small knife detaches
cream from side of
ramekin

4 Bake the creams until they are just set and the tip of the small knife inserted in the centre comes out clean, 20-25 minutes. Take the ramekins from the hot water bath and let them cool. Chill at least 2 hours.

! TAKE CARE !
Do not overcook the creams or they will curdle.

5 Just before serving, unmould the caramel creams: run a knife around the edge of each ramekin, then invert each cream onto a plate, allowing the sauce to pool around the cream. Serve chilled.

Caramel sauce is
perfect partner for
orange cream

Curled orange slice
is pretty decoration

VARIATION

LIME CARAMEL CREAMS

The tangy and refreshing flavour of lime combines deliciously with a light golden caramel in this variation of Orange Caramel Creams.

1 Make the caramel as directed, cooking it to a light golden brown.
2 Make the cream mixture as directed, using the juice from 6-7 limes with 250 ml (8 fl oz) water and 200 g (6½ oz) sugar.
3 Decorate the unmoulded creams with triangles of sliced lime.

RASPBERRY BAVARIAN CAKE

 SERVES 8 WORK TIME 55-60 MINUTES* 🍲 BAKING TIME 20-25 MINUTES

EQUIPMENT

pie slice

small knife

pastry brush

food processor

electric mixer

bowls

wooden spoon

parchment paper

sieve

25 cm (10 inch) cake tin

piping bag and star nozzle

23 cm (9 inch) springform tin

wire rack

saucepans

large serrated knife

rubber spatula

palette knife

INGREDIENTS

raspberries   egg yolks

caster sugar   gelatine

double cream   milk

butter   eggs

cornflour   vanilla pod

plain flour

kirsch   mint sprigs

Fresh raspberry purée flavours a Bavarian cream, sandwiched between rounds of sponge cake, and served with a kirsch-flavoured custard. When raspberries are not in season you can use frozen berries, though they lack the perfume of fresh.

* plus at least 4 hours chilling time

metric	SHOPPING LIST	imperial
	For the sponge cake	
	butter, flour, and vegetable oil for tins	
60 g	butter	2 oz
125 g	plain flour	4 oz
	salt	
4	eggs	4
135 g	caster sugar	4$^1/_2$ oz
30 ml	kirsch	2 tbsp
	For the raspberry Bavarian cream	
500 g	raspberries	1 lb
45 ml	kirsch	3 tbsp
200 g	caster sugar	6$^1/_2$ oz
250 ml	double cream	8 fl oz
1 litre	milk	1$^2/_3$ pints
1	vanilla pod or 10 ml (2 tsp) vanilla essence	1
10	egg yolks	10
45 ml	cornflour	3 tbsp
10 g	powdered gelatine	$^1/_3$ oz
60 ml	water	4 tbsp
	fresh mint sprigs for decoration	
	For the Chantilly cream	
175 ml	double cream	6 fl oz
15-30 ml	caster sugar	1-2 tbsp
15 ml	kirsch	1 tbsp

ORDER OF WORK

1 **MAKE THE SPONGE CAKE ROUNDS**

2 **MAKE THE RASPBERRY BAVARIAN CREAM**

3 **UNMOULD AND DECORATE THE CAKE**

1 MAKE THE SPONGE CAKE ROUNDS

1 Heat the oven to 220°C (425°F, Gas 7). Brush the cake tin with melted butter. Line the bottom with a round of parchment paper and butter the paper. Sprinkle in about 30-45 ml (2-3 tbsp) flour and turn and shake the tin to coat it evenly.

2 Melt the butter in a small pan and let it cool. Meanwhile, sift the flour and a pinch of salt into a bowl.

3 Put the eggs in a separate large bowl and beat a few seconds just to mix. Beat in the sugar.

4 Beat at high speed until the mixture leaves a ribbon trail when the beaters are lifted, about 5 minutes.

ANNE SAYS
"You can use a balloon whisk instead of the electric mixer, but heat will be needed to achieve volume. Set the bowl over a pan of hot, not boiling, water, and whisk vigorously, about 10 minutes."

5 Sift about one-third of the flour mixture over the egg mixture and fold them together as lightly as possible. Add the remaining flour in the same way in 2 batches.

6 Just after folding in the flour, pour in the cooled melted butter and fold it in gently but quickly.

ANNE SAYS
"Pour melted butter in a thin, steady stream while folding it in with the rubber spatula."

7 Pour the batter into the prepared cake tin and tap the tin on the work surface to level the batter and knock out air bubbles. Bake at once near the bottom of the heated oven, until the cake has risen and is just firm to the touch, 20-25 minutes.

Hold cake tin and wire rack together firmly

8 Turn out the cake onto the wire rack. Let cool, then carefully peel off the lining paper from the base of the cake.

9 Cut a thin slice from the top and bottom of the cake to remove the browned and marked portions; discard.

10 Cut the cake horizontally in half, using the serrated knife.

11 Trim the cake rounds to fit the springform tin, using the base of the tin as a guide.

12 Lightly oil the bottom and side of the springform tin.

ANNE SAYS
"It is best to use a good-quality stainless steel tin for making this cake, to avoid discolouring the Bavarian cream filling. To be extra sure, you can line the tin with cling film."

Sprinkle cake evenly with kirsch

13 Put one cake round in the bottom of the tin and sprinkle it with 15 ml (1 tbsp) of the kirsch. Set aside while making the Bavarian cream.

! TAKE CARE !
Prepare the cake and tin in advance to be ready for the Bavarian cream because it sets quickly.

2 MAKE THE RASPBERRY BAVARIAN CREAM

Purée raspberries for Bavarian cream all at once

1 Pick over the raspberries and set aside about one-quarter. Purée the rest in the food processor or in a blender, then work the puréed fruit through the sieve to remove the pips. There should be 375 ml (12 fl oz) of purée. Stir in 15 ml (1 tbsp) of the kirsch with 100 g (3½ oz) sugar, or more to taste.

2 Pour the cream into a chilled bowl and whip until it forms soft peaks and just holds a shape.

3 Put the milk in a medium saucepan. Split the vanilla pod, if using, and add it to the milk. Bring just to a boil. Remove the pan from the heat, cover, and let stand in a warm place, 10-15 minutes. Remove the vanilla pod from the milk. Rinse the vanilla pod and store to use again.

4 Set aside one-quarter of the milk. Stir remaining sugar into the hot milk in the pan, until dissolved.

6 Pour the egg yolk and milk mixture back into the saucepan and cook over medium heat, stirring constantly with the wooden spoon, until the custard comes just to a boil and is thick enough to coat the back of the spoon. Stir in the reserved milk and the vanilla essence, if using.

ANNE SAYS
"When the custard is thick enough, your finger will leave a clear trail across the back of the spoon."

5 Beat the egg yolks with the cornflour in a medium bowl. Add the sweetened hot milk and whisk until the mixture is smooth.

! TAKE CARE !
Do not overwhisk or the finished custard will be frothy instead of smooth.

Stir melted gelatine into custard with rubber spatula

7 Strain the custard into 2 medium bowls, dividing it equally. Let cool until tepid, then stir 30 ml (2 tbsp) kirsch into one half. Set this kirsch custard aside to serve with the finished dessert.

8 Sprinkle the gelatine over the water in a small saucepan and let soften, about 5 minutes. Set the pan over low heat and shake it occasionally until the gelatine is melted and pourable, 1-2 minutes; do not stir. Stir into the bowl of unflavoured custard.

9 Pour the raspberry purée into the unflavoured custard, stirring gently until evenly mixed.

10 Set the bowl in a large bowl of iced water. Stir the mixture until it starts to thicken. Remove the bowl from the iced water immediately.

11 Fold the raspberry custard into the whipped cream.

Raspberries will sink a little into the cream

12 Pour half of the Bavarian cream into the prepared cake tin.

13 Sprinkle the reserved whole raspberries on top, saving 8 for decoration. Pour the remaining Bavarian cream over the berries.

14 Evenly sprinkle the remaining 15 ml (1 tbsp) kirsch over the second cake round.

Sprinkling with kirsch ensures that cake round will be moist

15 Lightly press the cake round, sprinkled-side down, on the cream. Cover with cling film and refrigerate until firm, at least 4 hours.

ANNE SAYS
"Putting the kirsch-sprinkled side of the cake on the Bavarian cream ensures the flavour is absorbed by the cream."

3 UNMOULD AND DECORATE THE CAKE

1 Take the cake from the refrigerator, uncover, and remove the side of the tin. Transfer the cake to a serving plate.

ANNE SAYS
"Use a large pie slice to help move the cake off its base."

Squeeze piping bag gently when piping

2 Make the Chantilly cream: pour the cream into a chilled bowl and whip until soft peaks form. Add the kirsch and sugar to taste and continue whipping until the cream forms stiff peaks. Using the palette knife, spread some of the Chantilly cream over the top of the cake.

3 Put the remaining Chantilly cream into the piping bag and pipe it decoratively on the top of the cake.

TO SERVE
Decorate the top of the cake with the reserved raspberries and the mint, and serve the kirsch custard sauce separately.

Raspberries and mint sprigs decorate Bavarian cake

── **GETTING AHEAD** ──
The dessert can be made up to 48 hours ahead and kept in the refrigerator; remove 1 hour before serving. Make the Chantilly cream not more than 2 hours before serving.

V A R I A T I O N

ORANGE BAVARIAN CAKE

In this delicious variation of Raspberry Bavarian Cake, the Bavarian cream is flavoured with orange zest and juice, with a piquant hint of Grand Marnier.

1 Make the sponge cake rounds and prepare the springform tin as directed, sprinkling the first cake round with 15 ml (1 tbsp) Grand Marnier.
2 Grate the zest from 1 orange and squeeze the juice from 3 oranges (there should be 250 ml/8 fl oz juice). Whip the cream, and soften 15 g ($^1/_2$ oz) powdered gelatine in 60 ml (2 fl oz) of the orange juice.
3 Make the custard sauce and divide it between 2 bowls. Stir 15 ml (1 tbsp) Grand Marnier into one half of the custard and set it aside for serving. Melt the gelatine and stir it into the unflavoured custard sauce with the remaining orange juice, the zest, and 15 ml (1 tbsp) Grand Marnier. Continue with the Bavarian cream as directed.
4 Finish the cake as directed, sprinkling the remaining round with 15 ml (1 tbsp) Grand Marnier.
5 Peel and segment 2 oranges, cutting down between the membranes. Unmould the cake and spread with all of the Chantilly cream. Decorate with the orange segments and serve the Grand Marnier custard sauce separately.

BLACKBERRY FOOL

EQUIPMENT

food processor

sieve

metal spoon

wooden spoon

whisk

fork

saucepans

bowls

rubber spatula

The name "fool" for this old English dessert dates back at least to the sixteenth century and probably comes from the French "fouler", meaning to purée a mixture. Fools are traditionally made with a tart fruit.

GETTING AHEAD
The fool can be made 2 days in advance and the flavour will mellow. Keep it, covered, in the refrigerator.

metric	SHOPPING LIST	imperial
500 g	blackberries	1 lb
60 ml	water	4 tbsp
60-75 g	caster sugar, more if needed	2-2½ oz
250 ml	double cream	8 fl oz
	fresh mint sprigs for decoration	
	For the pastry cream	
375 ml	milk	12 fl oz
1	vanilla pod or 10 ml (2 tsp) vanilla essence	1
5	egg yolks	5
60 g	caster sugar	2 oz
30 g	plain flour	1 oz
	knob of unsalted butter	

INGREDIENTS

blackberries

caster sugar

double cream

milk

vanilla pod

egg yolks

butter

plain flour

fresh mint

ORDER OF WORK

1 PREPARE THE BLACKBERRY PUREE

2 MAKE THE PASTRY CREAM

3 FINISH THE FOOL

1 PREPARE THE BLACKBERRY PUREE

1 Pick over the blackberries and set aside 8 for decoration. Put the berries in a saucepan with the water.

2 Simmer over medium heat, stirring, until soft, but of a thick consistency, 8-10 minutes.

3 Transfer the berries and liquid to the food processor and purée to a fairly coarse texture.

Use wooden spoon to press purée through sieve

4 Press the purée through the sieve to remove the pips. There should be 375 ml (12 fl oz) of purée.

5 Stir in sugar to taste and set the purée aside to cool.

ANNE SAYS
"Flavours will blend and develop as the purée cools."

2 MAKE THE PASTRY CREAM

Split vanilla pod lengthwise in half before adding to milk

1 Put the milk in a small saucepan and add the split vanilla pod, if using. Bring to a boil, then remove from the heat, cover, and let stand, 10-15 minutes.

2 In a large bowl, whisk the egg yolks, sugar, and flour just to mix.

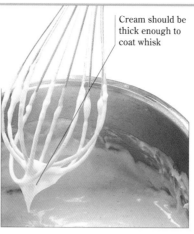

Cream should be thick enough to coat whisk

3 Whisk the hot milk into the egg yolk mixture until all the ingredients are thoroughly combined.

4 Return the mixture to the pan and cook over low heat, whisking constantly, until the flour has cooked and the pastry cream has thickened, 2-3 minutes. Simmer the cream over low heat 2 minutes longer.

5 Transfer the pastry cream to a bowl and remove the vanilla pod, if using, or stir in the vanilla essence. Using the fork, rub the butter over the surface of the cream to prevent a skin from forming. Set aside to cool.

3 FINISH THE FOOL

1 Pour the cream into a chilled bowl and whip until stiff peaks form and the whisk leaves clear marks in the cream. Set aside.

ANNE SAYS
"*If the kitchen is hot, set the bowl over iced water.*"

2 Add the blackberry purée to the cooled pastry cream and stir in with the rubber spatula to mix thoroughly.

3 Fold in the whipped cream gently. Cut down into the centre with the spatula, scoop under contents and turn over in a rolling motion. Taste; add more sugar if necessary.

Rubber spatula is excellent for folding mixtures together

4 Spoon the fool into stemmed glasses. If you like, mark a pattern on the surface of each fool. Cover and chill at least 2 hours.

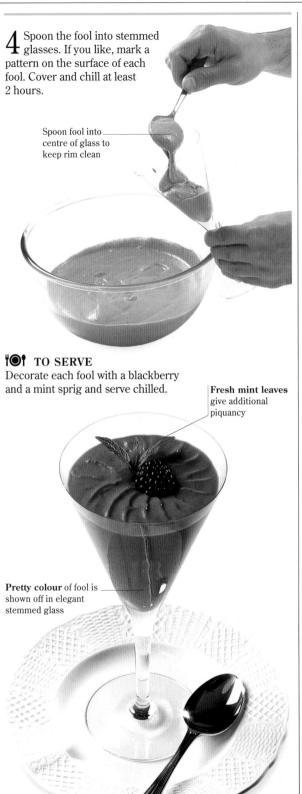

Spoon fool into centre of glass to keep rim clean

¶◎¶ TO SERVE
Decorate each fool with a blackberry and a mint sprig and serve chilled.

Fresh mint leaves give additional piquancy

Pretty colour of fool is shown off in elegant stemmed glass

VARIATIONS
REDCURRANT FOOL

Redcurrants are a natural for a fool, with cranberries a more unusual alternative. Both need more sugar than blackberries, so be sure to taste the fruit purée after adding the pastry cream.

1 Pick over 500 g (1 lb) redcurrants or cranberries. If using redcurrants, set aside 8 small bunches for garnish and pull the stalks from the remaining redcurrants with the tines of a fork.
2 Simmer the fruit with the water as directed until soft, 6-8 minutes. Continue as directed, adding sugar to taste.
3 Spoon the fool into stemmed glasses and chill.
4 Top with the reserved redcurrants and tiny mint sprigs, or sprinkle cranberry fool with ground cinnamon to serve.

RHUBARB FOOL

The tartness of rhubarb is ideal for fools. Strips of stem ginger make an attractive decoration, with a crisp brandy snap on the side.

1 Trim 375 g (12 oz) rhubarb stalks and wash them thoroughly.
2 Cut stalks into 2.5 cm (1 inch) pieces. Simmer with the water as directed until tender, 10-12 minutes. The coarse texture of the rhubarb is important in this dessert: do not purée. Stir in 100 g (3½ oz) sugar; add more if needed, to taste.
3 With a fork, crush the rhubarb against the side of the pan. Transfer the rhubarb to a bowl. Continue as directed.
4 Decorate the fools with stem ginger, if you like. Serve chilled.

POIRES BELLE HELENE

EQUIPMENT

- slotted spoon
- ice-cream maker
- vegetable peeler
- heavy-based saucepans, 1 with lid
- small ladle
- large shallow pan
- kitchen scissors
- ice-cream scoop
- wooden spoon
- whisk
- sieve
- bowls
- lemon squeezer
- chef's knife
- parchment paper
- small knife
- rubber spatula
- chopping board

This dessert of poached pears, vanilla ice cream, and hot chocolate sauce dates from the nineteenth century, when it was created for the star of Offenbach's opera, "La Belle Hélène".

GETTING AHEAD

A good dessert to prepare ahead: the ice cream can be made and frozen up to 2 weeks in advance. The chocolate sauce can be refrigerated, and the pears kept, covered in their poaching liquid, in the refrigerator, up to 3 days.

*plus 4 hours freezing time for the ice cream

metric	SHOPPING LIST	imperial
2	lemons	2
6	firm pears, total weight about 750 g (1½ lb)	6
750 ml	water	about 1¼ pints
1	vanilla pod	1
150 g	caster sugar	5 oz
	fresh mint sprigs for decoration	
	For the vanilla ice cream	
625 ml	milk	1 pint
1	vanilla pod	1
150 g	caster sugar	5 oz
8	egg yolks	8
30 ml	cornflour	2 tbsp
250 ml	double cream	8 fl oz
	For the chocolate sauce	
250 g	plain chocolate	8 oz
125 ml	water	4 fl oz
15 ml	brandy	1 tbsp

INGREDIENTS

pears

fresh mint sprigs

plain chocolate

caster sugar

vanilla pods

brandy

milk

egg yolks

double cream

lemons

cornflour

ORDER OF WORK

1 MAKE THE ICE CREAM

2 POACH THE PEARS

3 MAKE THE CHOCOLATE SAUCE AND FINISH THE DISH

1 MAKE THE ICE CREAM

1 Put the milk in a medium saucepan. Split the vanilla pod (see box, page 63) and add it to the milk. Bring the milk just to a boil. Remove from the heat, cover, and let stand in a warm place, 10-15 minutes. Remove the vanilla pod.

2 Set aside one-quarter of the flavoured milk. Add the sugar to the remaining flavoured warm milk and stir, with the wooden spoon, until all the sugar has dissolved.

3 Put the egg yolks with the cornflour into a medium bowl. Whisk them together until the mixture is smooth.

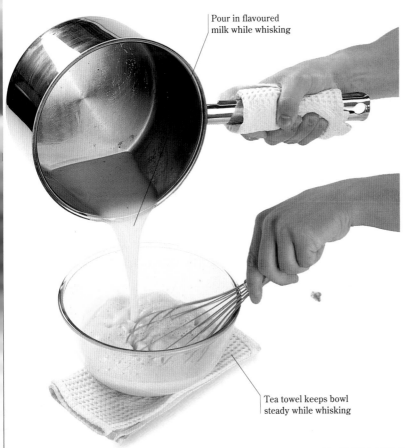

Pour in flavoured milk while whisking

Tea towel keeps bowl steady while whisking

4 Pour the sweetened flavoured milk into the egg yolk mixture, whisking until just smooth.

! TAKE CARE !
Do not overwhisk or the finished custard will be frothy instead of smooth.

5 Cook the custard over medium heat, stirring constantly with the wooden spoon, until it comes just to a boil and thickens enough to coat the back of the spoon. Your finger will leave a clear trail across the spoon.

! TAKE CARE !
Do not continue to boil the custard or it may curdle.

Straining ensures
custard is smooth

6 Add the reserved flavoured milk to the custard and stir continuously with the wooden spoon to combine, until it comes back to the boil.

7 Strain the custard into a cold bowl and leave it to cool completely. If it forms a skin, whisk to dissolve it.

8 Pour the vanilla custard into the ice-cream maker and freeze until slushy, following the manufacturer's directions. Meanwhile, chill a large bowl in the freezer.

9 Pour the cream into another chilled bowl and whip until soft peaks form.

Rubber spatula is efficient tool for transferring cream

10 Add the whipped cream to the half-set vanilla custard and continue freezing until firm.

Ice-cream maker will mix cream into custard

11 Transfer the ice cream to the chilled bowl, cover it, and freeze at least 4 hours. If you make the ice cream well ahead of time, put it in the refrigerator to let it soften, about 30 minutes before scooping.

2 POACH THE PEARS

Vegetable peeler circles neatly round core

1 Cut one of the lemons in half. Peel a pear, leaving the stalk intact.

2 Rub the cut surface of the lemon all over the peeled pear to prevent discoloration.

3 Working from the bottom, scoop out the pips and fibrous core from the pear using the vegetable peeler, without breaking open the fruit. Repeat with the remaining pears.

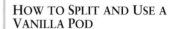

Intact stalk preserves character of pear

HOW TO SPLIT AND USE A VANILLA POD

Vanilla pods are used to flavour hot liquids such as milk and sugar syrup. The pods should be split open before use, so the seeds are exposed.

Thinly pared zest leaves pith behind

4 Pare the zest from the second lemon with the vegetable peeler. Squeeze the juice from the lemon.

Cut the vanilla pod lengthwise in half to expose the flavourful seeds. Add the pod to the liquid and bring it just to a boil. Remove from heat, cover, and let stand 10-15 minutes. To give a stronger vanilla flavour, remove the pod from the liquid, scrape out the seeds onto a board, and then return the seeds to the liquid and let stand 10 minutes more. Rinse the vanilla pod, dry, and store to use again.

5 Make the poaching syrup: combine the water, vanilla pod, if using, lemon zest and juice, and sugar in the shallow pan.

Add sugar all at once

Use pan that will hold all pears in single layer

6 Heat the mixture until the sugar has dissolved, then bring to a boil.

7 Remove the pan from the heat. Carefully add the whole pears to the poaching syrup.

ANNE SAYS
"The pears should be completely covered by syrup, so if necessary add more water to cover them."

8 Cut a disk of parchment paper the same diameter as the pan. Dampen it, then place it on top of the pears to keep them submerged in the syrup.

Discard parchment paper once pears are cooked

Do not cut into pears too deeply when testing if tender

9 Simmer the pears gently over low heat until tender when pierced with a small knife, 25-35 minutes, depending on ripeness. Let the pears cool in the liquid.

! TAKE CARE !
Do not let the liquid boil or the outside of the pears will disintegrate before the inside is cooked.

3 MAKE THE CHOCOLATE SAUCE AND FINISH THE DISH

POACHED PEAR FANS WITH CHOCOLATE SAUCE

Pear "fans" make a pretty presentation on a pool of cream, with chocolate sauce as a finishing touch.

1 Cut the chocolate into large chunks. Chop them with the chef's knife or in a food processor, using the pulse button. Combine the water and chocolate in a small saucepan. Stir over gentle heat until the chocolate is melted and smooth.

2 Simmer until slightly thickened and the consistency of double cream, 2-3 minutes. Remove from the heat, stir in the brandy, and keep the sauce warm.

3 Drain the pears well. Set a pear in the centre of each of 6 chilled serving plates. Arrange 5 scoops of vanilla ice cream around each pear. Ladle some warm chocolate sauce over the pears, decorate with mint, and serve at once. Pass the remaining sauce separately.

Warm chocolate sauce runs smoothly onto pear

Poached pear looks attractive with chocolate sauce poured sparingly on top

Mint leaves introduce green accent

1 Poach the pears and make the chocolate sauce as directed; omit the vanilla ice cream.
2 Cut each pear lengthwise in half, then cut each half lengthwise into slices, keeping the slices attached to the stalk. Press down gently with your fingertips on each pear half to separate the slices slightly.
3 Spoon 30-45 ml (2-3 tbsp) double cream onto 6 dessert plates and tilt them to spread out the cream into a pool. Arrange 2 pear halves on each plate, fanning out the slices.
4 Drizzle sauce in a wavy line onto each plate. To feather, draw the tip of a small knife across at intervals.

5 Spoon some chocolate sauce onto each pear half, near the stalk.

BAKED PEACHES WITH AMARETTI

🍽 SERVES 6   🥄 WORK TIME 15-20 MINUTES   🍲 BAKING TIME 1-1¼ HOURS

EQUIPMENT

slotted spoon

small knife

food processor   metal spoon

whisk*

bowls   medium saucepan

baking dish

chopping board

rubber spatula

* electric mixer can also be used

INGREDIENTS

peaches

Amaretti   unsalted butter

caster sugar

egg yolk

double cream   Amaretto liqueur*

fresh mint sprigs

* kirsch can also be used

ORDER OF WORK

1 PREPARE THE FILLING

2 PREPARE, FILL, AND BAKE THE PEACHES

A classic dessert from northern Italy, as delicious as it is easy to prepare, this can be served hot or cold. Amaretti, with their hint of bitter almonds, pick up the sweetness of the peaches, but macaroons can be substituted. The peaches should be ripe and full of juice, with no green tinge, or bruised or wrinkled skin.

GETTING AHEAD

The peaches can be baked ahead and kept up to 1 day in the refrigerator. Serve them cold, or cover and reheat them in a 180°C (350°F, Gas 4) oven about 15 minutes.

metric	SHOPPING LIST	imperial
7	large peaches, total weight about 1 kg (2 lb)	7
8-10	Amaretti	8-10
60 g	caster sugar	2 oz
1	egg yolk	1
	unsalted butter for baking dish	
	fresh mint sprigs for decoration	
	For the Chantilly cream	
125 ml	double cream	4 fl oz
15-30 ml	caster sugar	1-2 tbsp
15-30 ml	Amaretto liqueur	1-2 tbsp

1 PREPARE THE FILLING

Use metal blade in food processor

1 Heat the oven to 180°C (350°F, Gas 4). Scald, stone, and peel one peach (see box, page 68). Put the Amaretti in the food processor and grind them finely; pour them into a bowl.

ANNE SAYS

"You can also put the Amaretti in a thick plastic bag and crush them with a rolling pin."

2 Put the 2 peeled peach halves in the food processor. Process the peach halves until they become a thick, smooth purée.

3 Transfer the peach purée to a large bowl, scraping it from the food processor with the rubber spatula.

4 Add the sugar, egg yolk, and Amaretti crumbs to the peach purée and mix together well.

Crushed Amaretti should be in fine, even crumbs so they will blend easily with sugar and egg yolk

HOW TO SCALD, STONE, AND PEEL A PEACH

1 Bring a small saucepan of water to a boil. Using a slotted spoon, immerse the peach in the boiling water, about 10 seconds.

2 With a slotted spoon, transfer the peach to a bowl of cold water.

ANNE SAYS
"This loosens the skin. If peaches are less ripe, leave in the boiling water longer."

3 With a small knife, cut the peach in half, using the indentation on one side of the peach as a guide.

4 Using both hands, give a quick, sharp twist to each half to loosen it from the stone.

ANNE SAYS
"If the peach clings, loosen the flesh from the stone with a knife."

5 Lift or scoop out the stone with a small knife and discard it.

6 Peel off the skin from the peach halves.

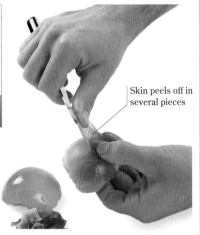

Skin peels off in several pieces

---

2 PREPARE, FILL, AND BAKE THE PEACHES

1 Butter the baking dish. Halve and remove the stone from the remaining peaches without peeling them. If necessary, with a spoon, scoopout a little of the peach flesh from the centre of each half so the cavity is large enough to hold the filling.

Use sharp-edged spoon to hollow out peach halves ready for filling

2 Set the peach halves, cut-side up, in the baking dish. Spoon some of the filling into each peach.

ANNE SAYS
"The peaches should fit tightly in the buttered baking dish."

HOW TO MAKE CHANTILLY CREAM

Chantilly cream is whipped double cream, lightly sweetened with sugar and flavoured with vanilla, brandy, kirsch, or other liqueurs and flavourings.

Pour the cream into a chilled bowl and whip until soft peaks form. Add the sugar and flavouring, and continue whipping until the cream forms stiff peaks.

🍽 TO SERVE

Transfer the hot peaches to individual serving plates, spoon any juices over the peaches, and decorate with mint sprigs. Serve the Chantilly cream in a separate bowl.

3 Bake the peaches in the heated oven until the peaches are tender, 1-1¼ hours. Meanwhile, make the Chantilly cream (see box, left).

Test peaches for tenderness by piercing flesh with tip of small knife

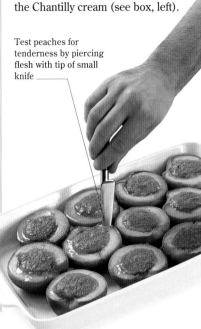

Amaretto and peach filling is bittersweet

BAKED FIGS WITH AMARETTI

Look for ripe figs with a sweet smell and no blemishes, for this variation.

1 With a small knife, trim the stalk ends off 14 ripe but firm, purple figs (total weight about 1 kg/2 lb).

2 Peel the skin from 2 of the figs using a small knife and purée the figs. Make the filling as directed, using the puréed figs and 6-8 Amaretti.

3 Cut a deep cross in the tops of the remaining figs, and open them by pushing the sides slightly.
4 Fill the figs and bake as directed, allowing 40-45 minutes.
5 Flavour the Chantilly cream with about 45 ml (3 tbsp) orange juice and 15-30 ml (1-2 tbsp) Grand Marnier or other orange liqueur.
6 Allowing 2 per person, serve the figs hot, with the orange Chantilly cream.

RASPBERRY SOUFFLE PUDDINGS WITH KIRSCH CUSTARD SAUCE

 SERVES 6 WORK TIME 20-25 MINUTES BAKING TIME 10-12 MINUTES

EQUIPMENT

6 medium ramekins
(225 ml/7 fl oz)

bowl sieves   conical sieve

pastry brush

whisk

wooden spoon

small ladle

heavy-based
saucepan

bowls   food processor*

rubber spatula

baking sheet

* blender can also be used

INGREDIENTS

raspberries

cornflour   kirsch

milk

egg yolks   egg whites

icing
sugar

butter

caster sugar

A hot, baked soufflé, and particularly this pudding version, need not be intimidating. What could be simpler than puréed fruit folded into meringue and baked? Here the puddings are served with a chilled custard sauce flavoured with kirsch. Given the few ingredients of this recipe, it is important that the raspberries be as sweet, juicy, and highly flavoured as possible.

GETTING AHEAD

The raspberry purée and kirsch custard sauce can both be prepared up to 1 day in advance and kept, covered, in the refrigerator. The egg whites must be whisked and the puddings baked just before serving.

metric	SHOPPING LIST	imperial
	unsalted butter and caster sugar for ramekins	
500 g	raspberries	1 lb
100 g	caster sugar, more if needed	3 1/2 oz
5	egg whites	5
30-45 ml	icing sugar for sprinkling	2-3 tbsp
	For the kirsch custard sauce	
375 ml	milk	12 fl oz
50 g	caster sugar	1 3/4 oz
5	egg yolks	5
15 ml	cornflour	1 tbsp
30-45 ml	kirsch	2-3 tbsp

ORDER OF WORK

1 MAKE THE KIRSCH CUSTARD SAUCE

2 PREPARE AND BAKE THE PUDDINGS

MAKE THE KIRSCH CUSTARD SAUCE

1 Pour the milk into the heavy-based saucepan and bring just to a boil over medium heat.

2 Set aside one-quarter of the milk to add later. Add the sugar to the remaining hot milk and stir until dissolved.

3 Put the egg yolks with the cornflour into a medium bowl. Whisk them together lightly, until the mixture is smooth.

4 Add the sweetened milk to the egg yolks, whisking until just smooth.

ANNE SAYS
"Do not overwhisk or the custard will be frothy instead of smooth."

5 Cook the custard over medium heat, stirring constantly, until it comes just to a boil and thickens enough to coat the back of the spoon. Remove from heat. Your finger will leave a clear trail across the spoon.

! TAKE CARE !
Do not continue to boil the custard or it may curdle.

Straining ensures custard is smooth

6 Stir the reserved milk into the custard, then strain it into a cold bowl and let it cool. If it forms a skin, whisk to dissolve it. Stir in the kirsch. Cover the custard tightly and refrigerate it while preparing and baking the soufflé puddings, about 25 minutes.

2 PREPARE AND BAKE THE PUDDINGS

1 Brush the ramekins with melted butter. Sprinkle each dish with caster sugar, tilting to coat the bottoms and sides evenly. Heat the oven to 190°C (375°F, Gas 5).

2 Pick over the raspberries, then purée them with half of the caster sugar in the food processor. Taste and add more sugar if the purée is tart.

3 Using the small ladle, work the purée through the conical sieve into a large bowl to remove the pips.

4 Whisk the egg whites until stiff. Sprinkle in the remaining caster sugar and continue whisking until glossy to form a light meringue, about 20 seconds.

Raspberry meringue mixture should have same texture as remaining meringue to make folding easy

5 Add about one-quarter of the meringue to the raspberry purée and stir the two together lightly, with the rubber spatula, to combine.

6 Add this mixture to the remaining meringue and fold together; cut down into the centre of the bowl with the rubber spatula, scoop under the contents and turn them over in a rolling motion.

7 Continue folding until the meringue is thoroughly incorporated into the raspberry purée and the mixture is an even colour.

Divide mixture evenly among ramekin dishes

8 Spoon the pudding mixture into the prepared ramekins. Set them on a baking sheet for easy handling. Bake in the heated oven until they are puffed and lightly browned on top, 10-12 minutes. Sprinkle the soufflé puddings with the icing sugar, using the sieve, and serve immediately, accompanied by the kirsch custard sauce.

Kirsch-flavoured custard sauce makes a delicate accompaniment

Icing sugar lightly dusted on top is finishing touch

V A R I A T I O N

STRAWBERRY SOUFFLE PUDDING WITH MINT CUSTARD SAUCE

Another red berry takes the stage here. If desired, make a diamond template to pattern the pudding with sugar.

1 Lightly crush a small bunch of fresh mint to develop the flavour.
2 Make the custard sauce, adding the mint to the hot milk, covering, and letting stand in a warm place, 10-15 minutes. Omit the kirsch.
3 Hull 300 g (10 oz) strawberries, washing them only if they are dirty, and purée them with sugar as directed. There is no need to strain the purée.
4 Prepare the pudding mixture as directed, using the strawberry in place of the raspberry purée, and bake in a prepared 1.5 litre (2½ pint) soufflé dish, allowing 15-20 minutes.
5 Serve immediately, with the mint custard sauce alongside.

FRUIT FRITTERS IN BEER BATTER WITH FRESH ORANGE SAUCE

🍴 SERVES 6-8   🥣 WORK TIME 20-23 MINUTES   🍲 FRYING TIME 30-35 MINUTES

EQUIPMENT

whisk*

2-pronged fork

vegetable peeler   apple corer

deep-fat thermometer if needed

small round pastry cutter

slotted spoon

chef's knife

paper towels

small saucepan

large metal spoon

sieve   bowls

deep-fat fryer**   chopping board

baking sheet
* electric mixer can also be used
**large pan can also be used

A light coating of batter allows fruit to be deep-fried while retaining its flavour and juice. The beer in the batter gives an especially crisp coating.

GETTING AHEAD

The fruit, batter, and sauce can be prepared and kept, covered, in the refrigerator up to 6 hours. Add the whisked egg whites to the batter and fry just before serving.

INGREDIENTS

oranges

bananas

light ale

pineapple

apples

egg

caster sugar

plain flour

orange marmalade

icing sugar

vegetable oil

egg whites

oil for deep-frying

metric	SHOPPING LIST	imperial
1	pineapple, weighing about 1 kg (2 lb)	1
4	tart apples, total weight about 750 g (1½ lb)	4
2	ripe bananas	2
	oil for deep-frying	
45-60 ml	icing sugar for serving	3-4 tbsp
	For the batter	
125 g	plain flour	4 oz
	salt	
1	egg	1
125 ml	light ale, more if needed	4 fl oz
2	egg whites	2
30 ml	caster sugar	2 tbsp
15 ml	vegetable oil	1 tbsp
	For the fresh orange sauce	
3	oranges	3
60 ml	orange marmalade	4 tbsp
15 ml	caster sugar (optional)	1 tbsp

ORDER OF WORK

1 **MAKE THE BATTER**

2 **MAKE THE FRESH ORANGE SAUCE**

3 **PREPARE THE FRUIT**

4 **DEEP-FRY THE FRITTERS**

1 MAKE THE BATTER

1 Sift the flour into a large bowl using the sieve or a flour sifter. Add the salt and make a well in the centre.

2 Add the whole egg and half of the beer to the well in the flour.

ANNE SAYS
"If too much liquid is added at this point, the batter will form lumps."

Continue whisking until batter is smooth

3 Mix with the whisk to make a smooth paste. Mix in the remaining beer. Cover and let stand at least 30 minutes.

ANNE SAYS
"The batter will thicken on standing."

2 MAKE THE FRESH ORANGE SAUCE

1 With the vegetable peeler, pare the zest from one of the oranges. Cut the zest into thin strips.

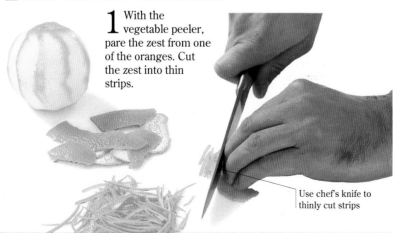

Use chef's knife to thinly cut strips

2 Put the zest in the small pan and add water to cover it generously. Bring to a boil and simmer 2 minutes. Drain, rinse under cold water, and drain again. Transfer to a bowl.

HOW TO PEEL AND SEGMENT CITRUS FRUIT

Seedless citrus fruit, such as navel oranges, are best for cutting into segments.

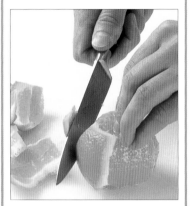

1 With a chef's knife, cut away both ends of the fruit just to the flesh. Set the fruit upright on a chopping board. Working from top to bottom using the same knife, cut away the zest, pith, and skin following the curve of the fruit.

2 Holding the fruit in your hand, slide the knife down one side of a segment, cutting it from the membrane. Cut down the other side and pull out the segment. Repeat with remaining segments, turning back the membrane like the pages of a book.

ANNE SAYS
"Segment the fruit over a bowl to catch the juice."

Tip orange segments and juice into bowl of orange zest

Orange segments should be free of all pith

3 Peel all 3 oranges with the chef's knife; working over a bowl, segment the oranges (see box, left), reserving the juice. Add the segments to the strips of orange zest.

4 Put the marmalade and orange juice in the small saucepan.

5 Heat gently until the marmalade is melted and smooth, stirring occasionally.

6 Let cool, then add to the orange segments and strips of zest and stir to mix. Taste the sauce and add sugar if needed, then chill until serving.

3 PREPARE THE FRUIT

1 Peel the pineapple and cut it into rings (see box, below). Peel the apples using the vegetable peeler. Force the apple corer into each apple, through the stalk end down to the base, and push out the cylinder containing the core and pips.

Corer removes apple core and pips neatly

Steady hand on work surface while coring apple

2 Cut the apples across into rings about 1 cm (½ inch) thick.

ANNE SAYS
"If preparing ahead, sprinkle the apples with lemon juice to prevent discoloration."

3 Peel the bananas; cut diagonally into 2.5 cm (1 inch) slices.

HOW TO PEEL PINEAPPLE AND CUT IT INTO RINGS

1 With a chef's knife, cut off the plume and base of the pineapple and set it upright, base-end down, on a chopping board. Cut away the peel in strips, working from top to bottom following the curve of the fruit and cutting deeply enough to remove the eyes with the peel.

Cut downwards and deep enough to remove all peel

2 Cut the pineapple across into 1 cm (½ inch) thick slices.

3 With a round pastry cutter, cut the core out of each slice.

4 DEEP-FRY THE FRITTERS

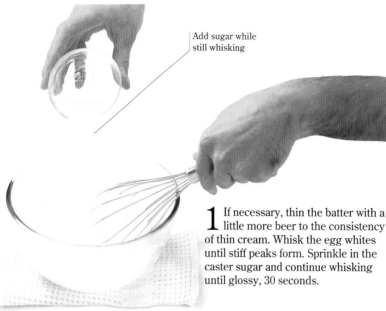

Add sugar while still whisking

1 If necessary, thin the batter with a little more beer to the consistency of thin cream. Whisk the egg whites until stiff peaks form. Sprinkle in the caster sugar and continue whisking until glossy, 30 seconds.

2 Add the egg whites to the batter and fold them together: cut down into the centre of the bowl with the large metal spoon, scoop under the contents, and turn them over in a rolling motion. At the same time, with your other hand, turn the bowl anti-clockwise. Continue folding until the egg whites are thoroughly incorporated.

Apple rings should have thin coating of batter

Fry only a few pieces at a time

3 Heat the oil in the deep-fat fryer to 190°C (375°F). Heat the oven to very low, for keeping the fritters warm.

ANNE SAYS
"To test the oil temperature without a thermometer, drop in a cube of bread: it should turn golden brown in 40 seconds."

4 Dip 4-5 apple rings in the batter so they are completely covered. With the 2-pronged fork, lift out one ring at a time and drain 1-2 seconds so excess batter drips into the bowl. Lower the ring gently into the hot oil, then add a few more rings, one at a time.

! TAKE CARE !
It is important to deep-fry in small batches so the fryer is not crowded and the oil temperature remains constant.

Lift fritters from fat with slotted spoon, tilting to pour off excess fat

5 Fry the fritters until crisp and brown on one side, 2-3 minutes, then turn with the slotted spoon and brown the other side.

6 Transfer the fritters to the baking sheet lined with several layers of paper towels. Keep warm in the oven with the door propped open. Dip and deep-fry the remaining apple, pineapple, and banana in the same way.

🍴 **TO SERVE**
As soon as all the fritters have been fried, arrange them on a serving plate, sprinkle with the icing sugar, and serve. Pass the fresh orange sauce separately.

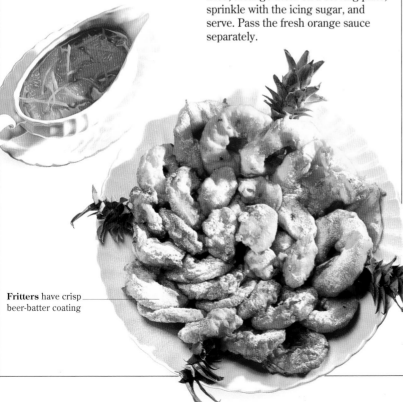

Fritters have crisp beer-batter coating

Pineapple tops make a pretty decoration

FRUIT FRITTERS IN CHAMPAGNE BATTER WITH RASPBERRY COULIS

Champagne or any sparkling white wine replaces beer in these light fruit fritters, with a tangy raspberry coulis as an accompaniment.

1 Make the batter as directed, replacing the beer with an equal quantity of Champagne or sparkling white wine.
2 Omit the fresh orange sauce and make a raspberry coulis: pick over 500 g (1 lb) fresh raspberries or use drained, defrosted fruit. Purée them in a food processor or blender. Stir in 15-30 ml (1-2 tbsp) kirsch, if you like, and add 30-45 ml (2-3 tbsp) icing sugar to taste. Work the purée through a sieve to ensure the coulis is smooth.
3 Prepare the fruit as directed.
4 Deep-fry the fritters and serve with the raspberry coulis.

CARIBBEAN FLAMBEED PINEAPPLE

 SERVES 6 WORK TIME 10-15 MINUTES ⛄ COOKING TIME 10-15 MINUTES

EQUIPMENT

2 cake tins

chef's knife

palette knife

large metal spoon

ice-cream scoop

small round
pastry cutter**   large frying pan

bowls

wooden spoon

chopping board

** small knife can also be used

Rings of fresh pineapple are sautéed with brown sugar and pecans, flamed with dark rum, and topped with desiccated coconut. Vanilla ice cream is a cooling accompaniment. When choosing a pineapple, give a quick tug to the plume – when ripe, the leaves should detach easily and the fruit should have a sweet odour. If you are short of time, commercial ice cream can replace the homemade vanilla ice cream (recipe on page 60).

GETTING AHEAD

The ice cream can be made up to 2 weeks ahead and kept in the freezer. The fruit can be prepared up to 4 hours ahead, then flambéed just before serving.

plus time for homemade ice cream

metric	SHOPPING LIST	imperial
1	pineapple, weighing about 1 kg (2 lb)	1
75 g	pecan halves	2¹/₂ oz
45 g	long-shred desiccated coconut	1¹/₂ oz
75 g	unsalted butter	2¹/₂ oz
100 g	soft brown sugar	3¹/₂ oz
75 ml	dark rum	2¹/₂ fl oz
	vanilla ice cream for serving	

INGREDIENTS

pineapple

vanilla
ice cream

desiccated
coconut

pecan halves

soft brown
sugar

unsalted butter

dark rum

ANNE SAYS
"If you are making your own ice cream, it will be very firm if made in advance, so let it soften in the refrigerator 30 minutes before serving."

ORDER OF WORK

1 PREPARE THE
INGREDIENTS

2 FLAMBE THE
PINEAPPLE

3 SERVE THE DISH

1 PREPARE THE INGREDIENTS

1 Heat the oven to 190°C (375°F, Gas 5). Cut the plume and base from the pineapple, then peel it, working from top to bottom following the curve of the fruit.

Use chef's knife to cut peel from pineapple

2 Cut the pineapple across into 12 thin slices and remove the cores with the pastry cutter.

Nuts are crisper when toasted

3 Put the pecans in one cake tin and the coconut in the other, spreading them both evenly.

4 Toast the pecans and coconut in the oven until golden, about 5 minutes, stirring occasionally with the wooden spoon so that they brown evenly. Let cool.

2 FLAMBE THE PINEAPPLE

1 Heat the butter in the frying pan until melted. Add the brown sugar.

Heat butter gently so it does not brown

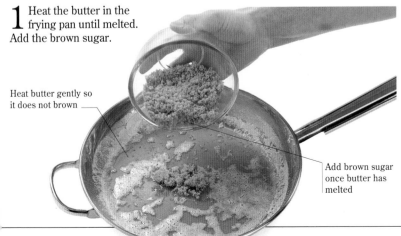

Add brown sugar once butter has melted

2 Cook over low heat, stirring with the metal spoon, until the brown sugar has melted, about 2 minutes.

3 Add the pineapple rings and cook until tender, 3-5 minutes, turning them once.

Turn pineapple rings with palette knife

ANNE SAYS
"The pineapple rings should lie flat in the pan so, if necessary, cook the rings in batches."

5 Turn the heat to medium high. Add the rum to the pan and bring the liquid to a boil.

Pour rum into simmering butter-and-sugar mixture

4 Sprinkle the toasted pecan halves on top of the pineapple rings.

Scatter nuts evenly in pan

6 Hold a lighted match to the side of the pan to set the rum alight. Baste the fruit with the sauce until the flames subside, 2-3 minutes.

! TAKE CARE !
Flames can rise quite high, so stand back and keep hair and face away from the flames. Use a long-handled metal spoon for basting.

SERVE THE DISH

1 Transfer 2 rings of pineapple to each serving plate and add a scoop of vanilla ice cream. Spoon the rum-and-pecan sauce over the pineapple. Sprinkle with the toasted coconut and serve immediately.

Fresh pineapple rings have a glaze of butter, brown sugar, and rum

Vanilla ice cream gives a cool and creamy touch

VARIATION

CHERRIES JUBILEE

Cherries Jubilee were created to commemorate Queen Victoria's golden jubilee.

1 Stone 500 g (1 lb) black cherries.
2 Cook the cherries in the butter and brown sugar, omitting the pecans and coconut, and use 75 ml (2½ fl oz) kirsch to flambé the cherries.
3 Put the cherries in 6 shallow bowls and top each with a scoop of vanilla ice cream. Spoon over the sauce and serve immediately.

VARIATION

FLAMBEED BANANAS FOSTER

This is a New Orleans dish, named after a local personality of the 1950s. Sugar-glazed almonds add texture and crunch to the softness of the bananas. Choose ripe bananas; their skins may have black spots, but there should be no large black patches.

1 Heat 45 g (1½ oz) raisins with 125 ml (4 fl oz) water in a saucepan until very warm. Remove from the heat, cover, and let soak 15 minutes. Drain them and discard the liquid.
2 To make sugar-glazed almonds for the topping, melt 15 g (½ oz) unsalted butter in a small frying pan and stir in 15 ml (1 tbsp) caster sugar. Add 30 g (1 oz) flaked almonds and cook gently, stirring occasionally, until the nuts are coated and browned, 2-3 minutes. Remove from the heat and sprinkle with 15 ml (1 tbsp) more caster sugar.
3 Peel 6 large ripe bananas and cut them crosswise in half. Cut each half lengthwise into 3-4 slices.
4 Cook the bananas in the butter and brown sugar as directed in the main recipe, sprinkling with 2.5 ml (½ tsp) ground cinnamon, and the soaked raisins instead of the pecan halves. When the bananas are tender, pour in the dark rum and flambé.
5 Serve as directed, sprinkling the sugar-glazed almonds over each serving in place of the toasted coconut.

GRATIN OF FRESH BERRIES WITH SABAYON

 SERVES 4 WORK TIME 15-20 MINUTES ♨ GRILLING TIME 1-2 MINUTES

EQUIPMENT

4 individual gratin dishes*

grater

—————— small knife

whisk

large saucepan

large metal spoon

bowls**   plate

baking sheet

*heatproof dessert plates can also be used

**to include 1 large heatproof bowl

In this dessert, a selection of fresh berries is topped with fluffy sabayon sauce flavoured with lemon zest and Grand Marnier or rich Marsala. Served in individual dishes, each gratin is grilled close to the heat to warm the fruit and give the sabayon an attractive golden-brown top. Professional chefs often save time by using a small blowtorch instead of the grill. Choose berries that are plump and full of colour.

GETTING AHEAD

The berries can be prepared, arranged in the dishes, and refrigerated 4 hours ahead. Sabayon sauce separates on standing, so it must be made and the dish grilled at the last minute.

INGREDIENTS

mixed berries

egg yolks

lemon

Grand Marnier***

caster sugar

***Marsala can also be used

ANNE SAYS
"Look for berries in season to achieve the full fruity fragrance of this sumptuous dessert."

ORDER OF WORK

1 PREPARE THE BERRIES

2 MAKE THE SABAYON

3 BROWN THE GRATIN

metric	SHOPPING LIST	imperial
375 g	mixed berries such as raspberries, strawberries, blackberries, blueberries	12 oz
1	lemon	1
3	egg yolks	3
50 g	caster sugar	1³/₄ oz
90 ml	Grand Marnier	3 fl oz

1 PREPARE THE BERRIES

1 Pick over the berries, washing them only if they are dirty. Hull the strawberries. Cut any large berries in half or into quarters.

Arrange berries attractively in individual dishes

2 Divide the berries evenly among the gratin dishes, arranging them decoratively, and chill in the refrigerator.

2 MAKE THE SABAYON

Combine ingredients in heatproof bowl to whisk over hot water later

1 Heat the grill. Grate the zest from half of the lemon.

ANNE SAYS
"Tap the grater firmly on the work surface to dislodge all the zest."

2 Put the egg yolks, sugar, and Grand Marnier in a large heatproof bowl and whisk them to mix.

3 Set the bowl over the saucepan half-filled with hot but not simmering water and start to whisk.

! TAKE CARE !
Make sure the bowl is large enough to sit in the saucepan without touching the water or the sauce will overheat and may curdle.

4 Continue whisking until the mixture is frothy and thick enough to leave a ribbon trail, 5-8 minutes. Take the sauce from the pan of hot water, whisk in the zest, and continue whisking 1-2 minutes until slightly cooled.

Mixture will become quite pale as it is whisked

3 BROWN THE GRATIN

1 Arrange the gratin dishes on the baking sheet and spoon the sabayon over and around the berries. Grill about 15 cm (6 inches) from the heat until the sabayon is golden brown and the fruit is warm, 1-2 minutes.

Berries are warm and succulent

🍽 TO SERVE
Transfer the hot dishes to plates for easy service and serve immediately.

Sabayon is grilled to deep golden brown

VARIATION
BERRIES AND ICE CREAM WITH SABAYON

1 Prepare the berries as directed.
2 Chill a large heatproof serving dish.
3 Take scoops from 1 litre (2 pints) vanilla ice cream and pile them in the dish.
4 Arrange the berries decoratively on top of the ice cream. Chill.

5 Peel the zest from the lemon with a vegetable peeler, instead of grating it, and cut it into thin strips.
6 Make the sabayon and spoon it over the fruit. Grill as directed and serve immediately. Serves 6-8.

HOW TO DESEED GRAPES

Many varieties of seedless grapes are now available, but if you have grapes with seeds, here are two ways to remove them quickly and easily.

To deseed with a paper clip: open a paper clip, insert the narrow end at the stalk end of the grape and twist to poke out the seeds.

To deseed with a knife: halve the grapes, then flick out the seeds with the tip of a small knife.

VARIATION
GRATIN OF CITRUS FRUIT AND GRAPES WITH SABAYON

This is a year-round variation of Gratin of Fresh Berries with Sabayon. The grapes should be firm and smooth.

1 Replace the berries with 4 medium navel oranges, 2 small grapefruit, and 90 g (3 oz) green or black grapes.
2 Cut away the skin and white pith from the citrus fruit, following the curve of the fruit. Cut out the segments, cutting down both sides of the dividing membrane. Drain the segments on paper towels.
3 Remove the stalks from the grapes and deseed them if necessary (see box, left).
4 Arrange the citrus segments in a flower-petal design in heatproof dessert dishes, with the grapes in a ring around the outside.
5 Make the sabayon sauce, omitting the lemon zest. Brown the gratins as directed.

AMERICAN PEACH PIE

🍴 SERVES 8   🥄 WORK TIME 40-45 MINUTES*   ♨ BAKING TIME 40-45 MINUTES

EQUIPMENT

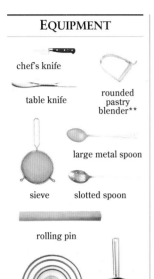

chef's knife

table knife

rounded pastry blender**

large metal spoon

sieve   slotted spoon

rolling pin

bowls   small saucepan

fork

pastry brush

23 cm (9 inch) pie tin

wire rack   small knife

baking sheet

cling film

**2 round-bladed knives can also be used

This is an American classic – ripe fresh peaches, their juice lightly thickened with flour and enclosed in a pastry lattice. When served "à la mode" with homemade vanilla ice cream, peach pie is the perfect summer dessert. Choose peaches that are ripe and full of juice, with no green tinge.

GETTING AHEAD
The pie can be made 1-2 days in advance and kept, covered, at room temperature, but it is best on the day it is baked.

plus 45 minutes chilling time

metric	SHOPPING LIST	imperial
	For the pastry dough	
250 g	plain flour	8 oz
2.5 ml	salt	1/2 tsp
125 g	white vegetable shortening	4 oz
75 g	unsalted butter	2 1/2 oz
45 ml	water, more if needed	3 tbsp
	For the filling	
4-5	fresh ripe peaches, total weight about 500 g (1 lb)	4-5
30 g	plain flour	1 oz
150 g	granulated sugar, more if needed	5 oz
	salt	
15-30 ml	lemon juice (optional)	1-2 tbsp
	For the glaze	
1	egg	1
2.5 ml	salt	1/2 tsp

INGREDIENTS

peaches

granulated sugar

vegetable shortening

egg

unsalted butter

plain flour

lemon juice (optional)

ORDER OF WORK

1 MAKE THE PASTRY DOUGH

2 LINE THE PIE TIN

3 PREPARE THE FILLING; BAKE THE PIE

1 MAKE THE PASTRY DOUGH

1 Sift the flour and salt into a large bowl using the sieve or alternatively a flour sifter.

2 Add the shortening and butter and cut them into the flour with the pastry blender.

3 Continue cutting until the mixture forms coarse crumbs.

Pastry blender is ideal utensil for mixing dough ingredients

4 Sprinkle with the water and continue blending until the dough can be gathered up into a ball. If too dry, add more water, a little at a time. Knead lightly until mixed, about 30 seconds.

5 Shape the dough into a ball, wrap tightly, and chill until firm, about 30 minutes.

2 LINE THE PIE TIN

1 Heat the oven to 200°C (400°F, Gas 6) and heat the baking sheet. Lightly flour the work surface and roll out two-thirds of the dough about 5 cm (2 inches) larger than the pie tin.

Rolling pin avoids need to handle pastry

2 Roll the dough around the rolling pin and drape it over the pie tin.

3 Lift the edge of the dough with one hand and press it well into the bottom of the tin with the other hand.

Reserve pastry trimmings to help make lattice

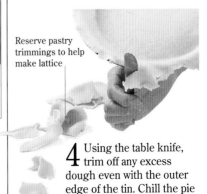

4 Using the table knife, trim off any excess dough even with the outer edge of the tin. Chill the pie shell 15 minutes.

3 PREPARE THE FILLING; BAKE THE PIE

Amount of sugar needed varies with ripeness of peaches

1 Immerse the peaches in boiling water and leave 10 seconds, then transfer to a bowl of cold water with the slotted spoon. Cut the peaches in half using the indentation on one side as a guide, remove the stone, and peel off the skin. Cut the peaches into 1 cm (½ inch) slices and put in a large bowl.

2 Sprinkle the peaches with the flour, sugar, a pinch of salt, and lemon juice to help cut the sweetness, to taste.

3 Carefully stir the peaches until they are coated with the sugar mixture, then transfer them to the lined pie tin with the juices in the bowl.

Lay strips over filling without stretching them

4 Press any dough trimmings into the remaining dough and roll it out into a rectangle. Cut out 8 strips 1 cm (½ inch) wide; reserve the trimmings.

5 Lay half of the strips from left to right across the pie about 2 cm (¾ inch) apart. Fold back every other strip halfway and place a fifth strip over the unfolded strips across the centre of the pie.

Arranging strips in this way gives lattice interwoven effect

6 Lay back the folded strips and fold back the alternates. Place the next strip about 2 cm (¾ inch) from the fifth. Continue until the pie is latticed. Turn the pie and repeat with the other half of the pie.

7 To make the glaze, in a small bowl, use the fork to beat the egg lightly with the salt. Trim the pastry strips even with the edge of the pie shell; reserve the trimmings. Moisten the ends of the strips with glaze and pinch with your fingers to seal them to the edge. Brush the lattice with glaze.

HOW TO MAKE PASTRY LEAVES

Pep up your presentation with a leafy border. Pastry leaves are very simple – and quick – to make.

Cut the dough into strips 2.5 cm (1 inch) wide, then cut diagonally across to make leaves. Mark veins on the leaves with the back of a knife. Curve the leaves with your fingers.

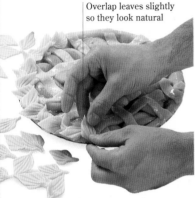

Overlap leaves slightly so they look natural

8 Re-roll the pastry trimmings and cut out leaves (see box, above). Lay the pastry leaves around the edge of the pie to cover the lattice ends.

9 Brush the leaves with glaze. Bake the pie in the oven on the heated baking sheet until the pastry is golden brown and the peaches are soft and bubbling, 40-45 minutes. Transfer the pie to the rack to cool slightly.

 TO SERVE
Serve individual pie portions warm or at room temperature.

Golden peaches peep through glazed lattice

V A R I A T I O N
CHERRY PIE

This most famous of all American pies is made just like Peach Pie.

1 Stone 500 g (1 lb) cherries.
2 Prepare the pie dough and line the pie tin as directed.
3 Stir the cherries with 200 g (7 oz) sugar, more if needed to taste, 45 g (1½ oz) flour, and 1.25 ml (¼ tsp) almond essence, if you like. Transfer the coated cherries to the lined pie tin.

4 Cut the pastry strips, using a fluted ravioli cutter, and use to make a lattice as directed in the main recipe. Cut 2 more strips with the ravioli cutter and lay them around the edge of the pie to cover lattice ends.

5 Flute the edge, pinching it with your fingers, and brush with glaze.
6 Bake the pie as directed. Serve at room temperature or slightly chilled.

NORMANDY PEAR TART

Tarte aux Poires Normande

🍴 SERVES 6-8 🥣 WORK TIME 40-45 MINUTES 🍲 BAKING TIME 40-45 HOURS

EQUIPMENT

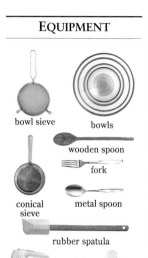

bowl sieve

bowls

wooden spoon

fork

conical sieve

metal spoon

rubber spatula

electric mixer

pastry scraper

food processor*

pastry brush

vegetable peeler

baking sheet

small saucepan

small knife

rolling pin

small ladle

thin knife

palette knife

melon baller

loose-based flan tin

* blender or rotary cheese grater can also be used

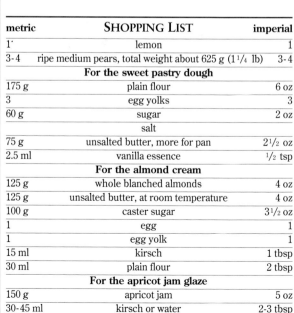

This delicious tart has become a signature recipe of Normandy. Sliced pears are arranged like petals and baked in almond cream. Pears should be ripe, or they will discolour during cooking.

GETTING AHEAD

The tart is best eaten the day of baking, although it can be kept up to 2 days in an airtight container.

INGREDIENTS

 pears

 egg yolks

 caster sugar

 egg

 lemon

 apricot jam

 unsalted butter

 kirsch

whole blanched almonds

plain flour

vanilla essence

metric	SHOPPING LIST	imperial
1'	lemon	1
3-4	ripe medium pears, total weight about 625 g (1¼ lb)	3-4
	For the sweet pastry dough	
175 g	plain flour	6 oz
3	egg yolks	3
60 g	sugar	2 oz
	salt	
75 g	unsalted butter, more for pan	2½ oz
2.5 ml	vanilla essence	½ tsp
	For the almond cream	
125 g	whole blanched almonds	4 oz
125 g	unsalted butter, at room temperature	4 oz
100 g	caster sugar	3½ oz
1	egg	1
1	egg yolk	1
15 ml	kirsch	1 tbsp
30 ml	plain flour	2 tbsp
	For the apricot jam glaze	
150 g	apricot jam	5 oz
30-45 ml	kirsch or water	2-3 tbsp

ORDER OF WORK

1 MAKE THE SWEET PASTRY DOUGH

2 LINE THE FLAN TIN

3 MAKE THE ALMOND CREAM

4 PREPARE THE PEARS

5 ASSEMBLE AND BAKE THE TART

1 MAKE THE SWEET PASTRY DOUGH

Pastry scraper is ideal tool for mixing dough

1 Sift the flour onto a work surface. Make a well in the centre and add the egg yolks, sugar, and a pinch of salt. Using the rolling pin, pound the butter to soften it slightly. Add the butter to the well with the vanilla.

2 Using your fingertips, work the ingredients in the well until thoroughly mixed.

3 Draw in the flour with the pastry scraper. With your fingers, work the flour into the other ingredients until coarse crumbs form. If they seem dry, add a little water.

5 Gather up the dough with the pastry scraper and continue to blend until it peels away from the work surface in one piece, 1-2 minutes. Shape into a ball, wrap tightly, and chill until firm, about 30 minutes.

! TAKE CARE !
Pastry doughs made with so much sugar are particularly delicate. Be sure to give the dough enough time to chill.

4 Press the dough into a ball. Lightly flour the work surface, then blend the dough by pushing it away from you with the heel of your hand.

2 LINE THE FLAN TIN

1 Brush the inside of a 23-25 cm (9-10 inch) flan tin with melted butter. Unwrap the dough; roll out on a lightly floured work surface to a round 5 cm (2 inches) larger than the tin.

Check size of rolled-out dough by placing flan tin on top

2 Roll up the dough around the rolling pin, then unroll it loosely over the flan tin.

Drape dough over tin without stretching it

3 Lift the edge of the dough with one hand and press it well into the bottom of the tin with the other hand. Leave a ridge of dough just inside the edge of the tin.

ANNE SAYS

"This ridge is pushed up over the edge of the tin to make a deep shell."

4 Roll the rolling pin over the top of the tin, pressing down lightly on the rolling pin to cut off the excess pastry dough. With your thumb, press the dough evenly up the side of the flan tin and above the top edge of the tin. Neaten the edge of the dough.

5 With both forefingers and thumbs, pinch the dough above the side of the tin to form a fluted edge. Prick the bottom of the tart shell with the fork to prevent air bubbles from forming during cooking. Chill the shell until firm, at least 15 minutes. Meanwhile, make the almond cream and prepare the pears.

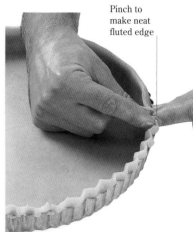

Pinch to make neat fluted edge

3 MAKE THE ALMOND CREAM

1 Grind the almonds in 2-3 batches in the food processor.

! TAKE CARE !

Do not overwork the nuts or their oil will be released, creating a paste.

Sprinkle sugar into softened butter

2 With the electric mixer or wooden spoon, cream the butter. Add the sugar and continue beating until fluffy and light, 2-3 minutes.

Beat in whole egg thoroughly before adding egg yolk

3 Add the egg and egg yolk to the mixture one at a time, beating well after each addition.

4 Add the kirsch, then stir in the ground almonds and flour.

4 PREPARE THE PEARS

1 Cut the lemon in half. Peel the pears with the vegetable peeler. As each pear is peeled, rub it all over with the cut lemon to prevent it from discolouring.

Melon baller cuts out core leaving neat hollow

3 With the small knife, cut the pears lengthwise in half. Neatly remove the core from the centre of each pear half with the melon baller or the tip of the vegetable peeler. Rub all the cut surfaces of each pear half with the cut lemon again.

2 Twist the stalk of each pear to remove it and scoop out the flower end with the tip of the peeler.

4 Set a pear half cut-side down on a chopping board. Using the thin-bladed knife, cut it lengthwise into thin slices, leaving them joined at the stalk end. Repeat with 6 more of the pear halves. Cut the last pear half crosswise into thin slices.

ANNE SAYS
"Each of the 7 fruit halves should hold together neatly after slicing."

HOW TO MAKE A FRUIT JAM OR JELLY GLAZE

A jam or jelly glaze is brushed on fruit to make it glisten and keep it moist. Make redcurrant jelly glaze to spread on red fruit; for other fruit, use apricot jam. A glaze can also give a protective coating to pastry, ensuring the filling does not seep in and make the pastry soggy.

1 Melt the jam or jelly with the water or other liquid in a small saucepan, stirring occasionally with a wooden spoon.

2 Work jam glaze through a sieve. Return to the pan and melt again over low heat.

ANNE SAYS
"If using a jelly it will not need to be sieved."

5 ASSEMBLE AND BAKE THE TART

1 Heat the oven to 200°C (400°F, Gas 6). Heat the baking sheet near the bottom of the oven. Spoon the almond cream into the chilled pastry shell and spread it evenly with the palette knife.

Smooth surface of almond cream layer

2 Flatten the 7 pear halves that were sliced lengthwise so that each has slightly overlapping slices.

Slide pear half from palette knife onto almond cream

3 Transfer the flattened pear halves to the tart using the palette knife, arranging them like the petals of a flower. Press them down lightly. Arrange the slices of the remaining pear half in the centre to resemble a rose.

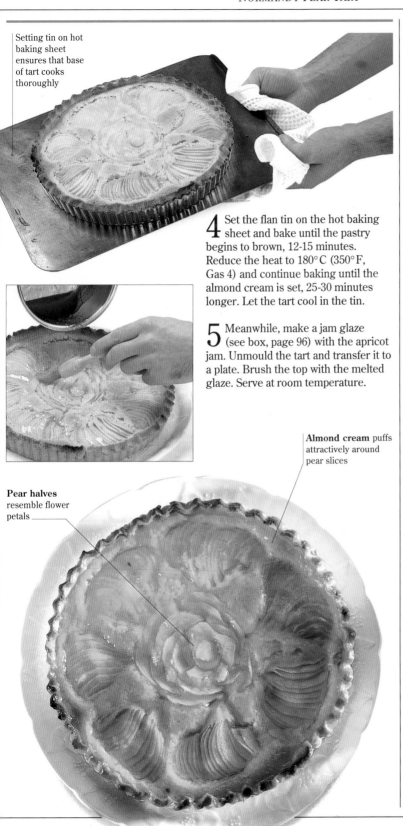

Setting tin on hot baking sheet ensures that base of tart cooks thoroughly

4 Set the flan tin on the hot baking sheet and bake until the pastry begins to brown, 12-15 minutes. Reduce the heat to 180°C (350°F, Gas 4) and continue baking until the almond cream is set, 25-30 minutes longer. Let the tart cool in the tin.

5 Meanwhile, make a jam glaze (see box, page 96) with the apricot jam. Unmould the tart and transfer it to a plate. Brush the top with the melted glaze. Serve at room temperature.

Almond cream puffs attractively around pear slices

Pear halves resemble flower petals

VARIATION
NORMANDY PEACH TART
Fresh, juicy peaches are used instead of ripe pears as the basis of this version of Normandy Pear Tart.

1 Make the sweet pastry dough and line the flan tin as directed in the main recipe. Make the almond cream.
2 Immerse 1 kg (2 lb) peaches in a pan of boiling water, leave 10 seconds, then transfer to a bowl of cold water. Cut each peach in half, remove the stone, and peel off the skin. Cut each half into thin slices and flatten them as for the pears, forming ovals.
3 Arrange the peach ovals on the almond cream.
4 Bake the tart as directed, and brush with the apricot jam glaze.

PHYLLO APRICOT TURNOVERS

🍽 MAKES 24   🥣 WORK TIME 35-40 MINUTES   ☕ BAKING TIME 12-15 MINUTES

EQUIPMENT

saucepans

small knife

chef's knife

grater

pastry brush

palette knife

plate

wire rack   sieve

wooden spoon

chopping board

bowl   tea towels

baking sheets

Phyllo is a multi-purpose dough, and not nearly as hard to work with as you might think. Here, phyllo is folded into triangles to enclose a filling of fresh apricots cooked with a spicy blend of cinnamon, nutmeg, and cloves. These light and flaky turnovers can be eaten with a knife and fork or your fingers.

GETTING AHEAD

The phyllo turnovers can be prepared, wrapped securely, and kept in the refrigerator up to 2 days; they also freeze well. Bake them just before serving.

metric	SHOPPING LIST	imperial
500 g	apricots	1 lb
1	lemon	1
200 g	caster sugar	6½ oz
5 ml	ground cinnamon	1 tsp
	ground nutmeg	
	ground cloves	
30 ml	water	2 tbsp
500 g	package phyllo dough	1 lb
175 g	unsalted butter	6 oz

INGREDIENTS

apricots

unsalted butter

lemon

phyllo dough

ground   ground
nutmeg   cinnamon

ground cloves

caster sugar

! TAKE CARE !
Do not allow phyllo to dry out or it will be impossible to fold. Work with one sheet at a time, keeping the rest covered with a moistened tea towel.

ORDER OF WORK

1 MAKE THE APRICOT FILLING

2 FILL AND SHAPE THE PHYLLO TURNOVERS

3 BAKE THE PHYLLO TURNOVERS

1 MAKE THE APRICOT FILLING

Use small knife to slice apricot halves

1 Cut each apricot in half around the stone. Using both hands, give a quick, sharp twist to each half to loosen it from the stone. Scoop out the stone with the knife and discard. Cut each half into 4-5 pieces. Grate the zest from half of the lemon onto the plate.

2 In a medium saucepan, combine the apricots, lemon zest, three-quarters of the sugar, the cinnamon, and a pinch each of nutmeg and cloves. Add the water.

3 Cook gently, stirring occasionally, until the mixture thickens to the consistency of jam, 20-25 minutes. Transfer to the bowl and let cool.

ANNE SAYS
"*Some apricots should stay in pieces to give the filling texture.*"

2 FILL AND SHAPE THE PHYLLO TURNOVERS

Fold phyllo carefully to avoid wrinkles and splitting

1 Heat the oven to 200°C (400°F, Gas 6). Lay a tea towel on the work surface and sprinkle it lightly with water.

2 Unroll the phyllo dough sheets on the towel and cut them lengthwise in half. Cover them with a second moistened towel.

3 Melt the butter in a small pan. Take one half sheet of dough from the pile and set it lengthwise on the work surface. Lightly brush half of the sheet lengthwise with butter and fold the other half on top.

Centre apricot filling
on dough strip

4 Brush the strip of dough with more butter. Spoon 5-10 ml (1-2 tsp) of the cooled filling onto the strip of dough about 2.5 cm (1 inch) from one end.

! TAKE CARE !
Do not put too much apricot filling in the turnovers or they will burst during cooking.

5 Fold a corner of the dough strip over the filling to meet the other edge of dough, forming a triangle.

6 Continue folding the strip over and over to form a triangle with the filling inside. Set the triangle on a baking sheet with the final edge underneath, and cover the baking sheet with a moistened tea towel.

ANNE SAYS
"Close the corners tightly so the filling does not leak."

Shape triangle gently
without squeezing it

7 Continue making triangles with the remaining phyllo dough and filling, arranging them on the baking sheets and keeping them covered with moistened tea towels.

3 BAKE THE PHYLLO TURNOVERS

1 Brush the top of each triangle with butter and sprinkle with the remaining sugar. Bake in the heated oven until golden brown and flaky, 12-15 minutes. With the palette knife, transfer the turnovers to the rack to cool slightly, and serve warm or at room temperature.

Sugar glaze gives crisp finish

Phyllo pastry is flaky and delicate

VARIATION
PHYLLO BERRY TURNOVERS

Mixed red berries replace the fresh apricots in Phyllo Apricot Turnovers.

1 Hull 250 g (8 oz) strawberries and pick over 175 g (6 oz) raspberries. Cut strawberries in half or into quarters. Put all the fruit in a bowl, sprinkle with 60 g (2 oz) sugar and toss lightly to combine.
2 Fill each triangle with 10-15 ml (scant 1 tbsp) berries. Brush with butter, sprinkle with sugar, and bake as directed.
3 Decorate each serving with raspberries and mint sprigs, if you like.

VARIATION
PHYLLO APRICOT PURSES

An attractive alternative to pastry triangles, here squares of phyllo dough are wrapped up around the apricot filling and the ends are lightly twisted to resemble a purse.

1 Make the apricot filling as directed.
2 Take 4 of the sheets of phyllo dough, keeping them in a stack. With a chef's knife, cut the layered sheets lengthwise, then crosswise to make 11 cm (4½ inch) squares. Discard any dough trimmings.
3 Keeping the remaining squares and uncut dough covered, place one square on the work surface and brush it with butter. Set a second square on top, at a 45° angle to the first, and butter it. Repeat to make a stack of 4 squares.
4 Spoon 5-10 ml (1-2 tsp) cooled apricot filling into the centre and pull the points of the squares up over the filling to make a purse. Twist it gently to seal the purse tightly.
5 Tie the purse closed with a small piece of string. Continue with the remaining stacks of squares, then repeat the process with the remaining sheets of dough and filling, to make 24 purses in all.
6 Bake as directed, then cut off the string. Serve on individual plates, with 3 warm apricot purses on each.

CARAMELIZED UPSIDE-DOWN APPLE TART

APPLE TART

Tarte Tatin

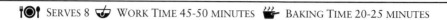

🍽 SERVES 8 🥄 WORK TIME 45-50 MINUTES ☕ BAKING TIME 20-25 MINUTES

EQUIPMENT

chef's knife

small knife

heavy-based deep frying pan, with metal handle (23-25 cm/ 9-10 inch diameter)

small plate

pastry scraper

medium saucepan

bowls

vegetable peeler

wooden spoon

large 2-pronged fork

melon baller

chopping board

palette knife

sugar thermometer

sieve

rolling pin

Tarte Tatin is named after two impoverished gentlewomen, from the French region of Sologne, who earned their living by baking their father's favourite apple tart. The secret of this upside-down tart lies in cooking the apples in the caramel itself, so it flavours deep inside the fruit. It is delicious served warm with crème fraîche.

GETTING AHEAD

The tart can be baked 6-8 hours ahead and kept at room temperature. Warm the tart briefly on top of the stove and unmould it just before serving.

metric	SHOPPING LIST	imperial
14-16	apples, total weight about 2.4 kg (5 lb)	14-16
1	lemon	1
125 g	unsalted butter	4 oz
200 g	caster sugar	6½ oz
	crème fraîche for serving (see box, page 106)	
	For the pastry dough	
75 g	unsalted butter	2½ oz
175 g	plain flour	6 oz
2	egg yolks	2
22.5 ml	caster sugar	1½ tbsp
	salt	
15 ml	water, more if needed	1 tbsp

INGREDIENTS

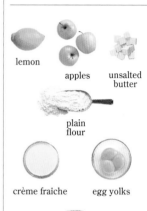

lemon

apples

unsalted butter

plain flour

crème fraîche

egg yolks

caster sugar

ANNE SAYS
"Crème fraîche is the ideal accompaniment for the caramel-steeped fruit tart. If you are baking ahead, make the crème fraîche at the same time, because its flavour takes 6-8 hours to develop."

ORDER OF WORK

1 MAKE THE PASTRY DOUGH

2 PREPARE AND CARAMELIZE THE APPLES

3 BAKE THE TART; UNMOULD

1 MAKE THE PASTRY DOUGH

Add other dough ingredients to well in flour

1 Using the rolling pin, pound the butter to soften it slightly. Sift the flour onto a work surface and make a well in the centre. Put the egg yolks, sugar, and a pinch of salt in the centre of the well, then add the softened butter and the water.

2 Using your fingertips, work the ingredients in the well until thoroughly mixed.

3 Draw the flour into the well using the pastry scraper. With your fingers, work the flour into the other ingredients until coarse crumbs form. If they seem dry, add a little more water. Press the dough into a ball.

Heel of hand only is used for blending dough

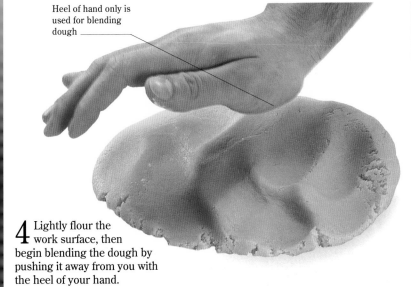

4 Lightly flour the work surface, then begin blending the dough by pushing it away from you with the heel of your hand.

5 Gather up the dough with the pastry scraper and blend until it is very smooth and peels away from the work surface in one piece, 1-2 minutes. Shape into a ball, wrap it tightly, and chill until firm, about 30 minutes.

HOW TO HALVE AND CORE AN APPLE

If you use the correct technique and equipment for preparing fruit, no matter how simple these are, you are more likely to get a professional finish.

1 With the point of a small, sharp knife, cut around the stalk end of the apple; remove the stalk. Repeat with the flower end.

2 With the same knife, cut the apple lengthwise in half.

3 With a melon baller, carefully scoop out the core and pips from the centre of each apple half, leaving as neat a shape as possible.

2 PREPARE AND CARAMELIZE THE APPLES

1 With the vegetable peeler or a small knife, carefully remove the outer peel from the apples in thin lengthwise strips. Halve and core the apples (see box, left).

2 Cut the lemon in half and rub the apples all over with the cut lemon to prevent discoloration.

Pour sugar into melted butter all at once

When butter starts to sizzle, add sugar

3 Melt the butter in the frying pan. Add the sugar.

Arrange second circle of apple halves facing in opposite direction to first

4 Cook over medium heat; stirring occasionally with the wooden spoon, until caramelized to a deep golden brown, 3-5 minutes. Remove from the heat and let cool to tepid.

! TAKE CARE !
Cook gently once the caramel starts to colour because it burns easily.

5 Arrange the apple halves upright in concentric circles to fill the pan. Prop up the first apple with the wooden spoon, then lean the others against it. The apples will shrink during cooking, so pack them tightly here.

Apple halves fit snugly into each other in pan

6 Cook the apples over high heat until caramelized, 15-25 minutes. Turn once to caramelize on both sides.

ANNE SAYS
"*Cooking time depends on the apples you use. When cooked they should be tender but still retain their shape, and very little juice should remain.***"**

Use 2-pronged fork to turn apples carefully

7 When the apples are completely caramelized, take the pan from the heat and let cool 10-15 minutes. Heat the oven to 190°C (375°F, Gas 5).

3 BAKE THE TART; UNMOULD

Roll up dough around pin, then unroll over frying pan

1 Roll out the pastry dough to a round about 2.5 cm (1 inch) larger than the frying pan. Roll up the dough around the rolling pin.

2 Drape the dough over the pan. Tuck the edges of the dough down around the apples. Bake the tart in the heated oven until the crust is golden brown, 20-25 minutes.

HOW TO MAKE CREME FRAICHE

When unpasteurized cream is left to stand, it develops a full, slightly sour taste. This is crème fraîche, the standard cream in France. Modern production methods use pasteurized cream that is recultured by adding bacteria to replace those destroyed by pasteurization. It can be purchased at some supermarkets, but if you find it difficult to obtain, it is easy to make with this recipe.

SHOPPING LIST

500 ml (16 fl oz) double cream
250 ml (8 fl oz) buttermilk or soured cream

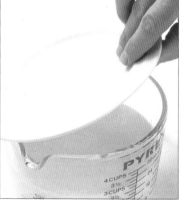

1 Pour the double cream into a medium saucepan, add the buttermilk or soured cream, and stir to mix. Heat gently to 24°C (75°F). Pour the mixture into a glass measuring jug or a bowl.

2 Cover with a plate, leaving a gap for air. Leave at room temperature (21°C/70°F), until the mixture has thickened and tastes slightly acid, 6-8 hours. Stir, then cover and refrigerate.

3 Let the tart cool to tepid in the pan, then unmould it: set a serving plate on top of the pan, hold firmly together, and invert the two. If any apples stick to the pan, remove and replace on the tart. Spoon some caramel from the plate over the apples. Serve with crème fraîche.

Lift pan away carefully so arrangement of apples is not disturbed

Caramel seeps through tart and forms a pool on plate

Apples are coated with caramel to give them a golden glow

VARIATION

CARAMELIZED UPSIDE-DOWN PEAR TART

Caramelized pears are just as delicious as apples in this variation of Tarte Tatin.

1 Peel, halve, and core 12-14 pears (total weight about 2.4 kg/5 lb).

2 Caramelize the pears as directed for the apples in the main recipe, arranging them on their sides in the pan with the tapered ends towards the centre of the pan.

3 Cover with the pastry dough. Bake the tart and unmould as directed.

ANNE SAYS
"*Pears may produce more liquid than apples and so take longer to cook in the caramel until the liquid has evaporated.*"

FRESH FRUIT TARTLETS

 SERVES 8   WORK TIME 40-45 MINUTES*   BAKING TIME 11-13 MINUTES

EQUIPMENT

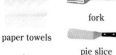

saucepans, 1 with lid

paper towels

fork

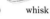

pie slice

8 (10 cm/4 inch) tartlet tins

whisk

small knife

cling film

pastry brush

sieve

slotted spoon

pastry scraper

small ladle

metal spoon

bowls

baking sheet

wire rack

aluminium foil

rolling pin

A crisp, sweet pastry shell lined with vanilla pastry cream is the ideal way to display the best of fresh fruit. Finished with a jam glaze, contrasting colours, such as red raspberries, golden peaches, and green kiwi fruit, look especially good. All fruit will look attractive, though; choose whatever is in season.

*plus 1 hour chilling time

INGREDIENTS

vanilla essence

mixed fresh fruit

apricot jam**

egg yolks

vanilla pod

unsalted butter

caster sugar

milk

plain flour

**redcurrant jelly is used if all fruit is red

metric	SHOPPING LIST	imperial
500 g	mixed fresh fruit, such as kiwi fruit, raspberries, grapes, peaches	1 lb
	For the sweet pastry dough	
175 g	plain flour	6 oz
4	egg yolks	4
90 g	caster sugar	3 oz
2.5 ml	salt	½ tsp
2.5 ml	vanilla essence	½ tsp
90 g	unsalted butter, more for tartlet tins	3 oz
	For the vanilla pastry cream	
375 ml	milk	12 fl oz
1	vanilla pod or 10 ml (2 tsp) vanilla essence	1
5	egg yolks	5
60 g	caster sugar	2 oz
30 g	plain flour	1 oz
	knob of unsalted butter	
	For the jam glaze	
175 ml	apricot jam or redcurrant jelly	6 fl oz
30-45 ml	water	2-3 tbsp

ORDER OF WORK

1 MAKE THE SWEET PASTRY DOUGH

2 MAKE THE PASTRY CREAM

3 LINE AND BAKE BLIND THE TARTLET SHELLS

4 PREPARE THE FRUIT AND GLAZE

5 ASSEMBLE THE TARTLETS

1 MAKE THE SWEET PASTRY DOUGH

Side of well must be high enough to contain ingredients in centre

1 Sift the flour onto a work surface and make a well in the centre.

2 Put the egg yolks, sugar, salt, and vanilla essence in the well in the centre of the sifted flour.

Softening butter makes it easy to blend with other ingredients

3 Using the rolling pin, pound the butter to soften it slightly and add it to the well.

4 With your fingertips, work the ingredients in the well until thoroughly mixed. Draw in the flour with the pastry scraper.

Work ingredients together before mixing in flour

5 With your fingers, work the flour into the other ingredients until coarse crumbs form. Press the dough into a ball.

6 Lightly flour the work surface, then blend the dough by pushing it away from you with the heel of your hand.

Gently knead dough just to mix it

7 Gather up the dough with the pastry scraper and blend until it is very smooth and peels away from the work surface in one piece, 1-2 minutes.

8 Shape the dough into a ball, wrap it tightly, and chill until firm, about 30 minutes.

! TAKE CARE !
Pastry doughs made with this quantity of sugar are particularly delicate. Be sure to give the dough enough time to chill.

2 MAKE THE PASTRY CREAM

1 Bring the milk to a boil in a saucepan with the split-open vanilla pod, if using. Remove the pan from the heat, cover, and let stand 10-15 minutes. In a bowl, whisk together the egg yolks, sugar, and flour just to mix.

Use large bowl to whisk mixture

Milk is flavoured with vanilla pod

2 Whisk in the hot milk until thoroughly combined. Return the mixture to the pan and cook over low heat, whisking constantly, until the flour has cooked and the cream is thick, 2-3 minutes. Simmer the cream over low heat 2 minutes.

ANNE SAYS
"Simmering the pastry cream cooks the flour so it leaves no aftertaste."

3 Transfer the pastry cream to another bowl and remove the vanilla pod if using, or stir in the vanilla essence. Rub the butter over the surface of the cream to prevent a skin from forming. Let cool.

3 LINE AND BAKE BLIND THE TARTLET SHELLS

1 Melt a little butter and use to brush the tartlet tins.

2 Lightly flour the work surface. Roll out the dough to a 3 mm (1/8 inch) thickness.

Unroll dough over tartlet tins

3 Group the tins together, with their edges nearly touching. Roll the dough loosely around the rolling pin and drape it over the tins so all are covered.

4 Tear off a small piece of dough from the edge, form it into a ball, dip it in flour, and use it to push the dough into the tins.

ANNE SAYS
"Brush off any excess flour from the dough."

Cut off excess dough with rolling pin

Neat, flat edge will be cut this way

5 Roll the rolling pin over the tops of the tins to remove excess dough. With your fingers, press up the dough edges to form a deep shell.

ANNE SAYS
"Excess pastry dough can be rolled out again and used to line any remaining tartlet tins."

6 Set the tartlet tins on the baking sheet and prick the dough with the fork. Chill the tartlet shells until firm, about 30 minutes. Heat the oven to 200°C (400°F, Gas 6).

Foil ensures that tartlet shell keeps its shape during baking

7 Line each tartlet shell with a piece of foil, pressing it down well.

ANNE SAYS
"Alternatively, omit the foil and line each tartlet shell with a tin of the same size, baking the dough in 2 batches."

8 Bake the shells in the heated oven until the pastry is set, 6-8 minutes. Remove the foil and continue baking until thoroughly cooked, about 5 minutes longer.

Handle tartlet shells with care so you do not damage them

9 With the pie slice, transfer the tartlet tins to the wire rack to cool. When cold, remove each tartlet shell from its tin.

4 PREPARE THE FRUIT AND GLAZE

1 Peel the skin off the kiwi fruit in strips, working from top to bottom following the curve of the fruit. Slice the fruit, then cut the slices into quarters. Pick over raspberries.

ANNE SAYS
"If using strawberries, hull them and wash them only if they are dirty; cut any large berries in half. Peel and segment tangerines, discarding any pips."

2 Remove stalks, then wash and dry the grapes. If the grapes are not seedless, remove the seeds with an opened paper clip (see box, page 87). Immerse peaches in a pan of boiling water, leave 10 seconds, then transfer with the slotted spoon to a bowl of cold water. Cut each peach in half, remove the stone, and peel off the skin. Cut the halves into slices.

3 Make the jam glaze, using apricot jam if the fruits are mixed in colour, or redcurrant jelly if they are all red fruit. Melt the jam or jelly with the water in a small saucepan. Work it through the sieve and melt again over low heat.

ANNE SAYS
"If using jelly, it will not need to be sieved."

5 ASSEMBLE THE TARTLETS

1 Brush the inside of each tartlet shell with the melted jam glaze.

2 Half fill each shell with the cooled pastry cream, smoothing the top with the back of the spoon.

Make decorative pattern with fruit

3 Arrange the fruit on top of the cream. Brush the fruit with the jam glaze.

Green fruit contrast with red and golden fruit

Jam glaze makes fruit glisten like jewels

VARIATION

FRESH FRUIT TART

This full-size tart offers a striking presentation of fresh fruit arranged in concentric circles over vanilla pastry cream.

1 Make and chill the pastry dough as directed. Roll out the dough to 3 mm ($^1/_8$ inch) thick and use to line a 25 cm (10 inch) pie tin. Prick the dough with a fork to prevent it from puffing during cooking. Chill until firm, about 30 minutes.

2 Line the pastry shell with a double thickness of foil, pressing it well into the bottom edge. Half fill the foil with dried beans or rice to weigh down the dough. Bake as directed, allowing about 15 minutes with the foil and beans; remove the foil and beans and bake 7-10 minutes longer.

3 Make the pastry cream, and prepare a selection of fresh fruit and a jam glaze as directed.

4 Brush the pastry shell with glaze, add the pastry cream, and top it with concentric rings of fruit. Glaze the fruit to finish.

ANNE SAYS

"Be sure the rings of fruit contrast in colour."

GETTING AHEAD

The tartlet shells can be baked 2 days in advance and stored in an airtight container. The pastry cream can be made 1 day ahead and refrigerated, tightly covered.

CHERRY STRUDEL

 SERVES 6-8   WORK TIME 45-50 MINUTES*   BAKING TIME 30-40 MINUTES

EQUIPMENT

palette knife**

chef's knife

cherry stoner

small saucepan

whisk

pastry brush

grater

sieve

bowls

tea towel

plate

chopping board

bed sheet

baking sheet

metal skewer

rolling pin

**pastry scraper can also be used

Don't be intimidated by making the ultra-thin strudel pastry; the trick is to knead the dough thoroughly so it is elastic. You will, however, need a large work table and a sheet to cover it.

GETTING AHEAD

Because strudel dough dries out easily, the strudel should be assembled and cooked at once. It is best eaten the day of baking, but can be kept in the refrigerator up to 24 hours. Reheat in a 180°C (350°F, Gas 4) oven, 10-15 minutes.

* plus 45 minutes resting time

INGREDIENTS

cherries   egg

light soft brown sugar   ground cinnamon   walnuts

lemon   caster sugar

unsalted butter   brandy***   double cream

icing sugar

lemon juice

plain flour

***or 5 ml (1tsp) vanilla essence

metric	SHOPPING LIST	imperial
1	lemon	1
500 g	cherries	1 lb
75 g	walnuts	2½ oz
100 g	light soft brown sugar	3½ oz
5 ml	ground cinnamon	1 tsp
	icing sugar for sprinkling	
	For the strudel dough	
250 g	plain flour, more if needed	8 oz
1	egg	1
125 ml	water	4 fl oz
2.5 ml	lemon juice	½ tsp
	salt	
125 g	unsalted butter, more for baking sheet	4 oz
	For the Chantilly cream	
250 ml	double cream	8 fl oz
30 ml	caster sugar	2 tbsp
30 ml	brandy	2 tbsp

ORDER OF WORK

1 MAKE THE STRUDEL DOUGH

2 PREPARE THE FILLING AND CHANTILLY CREAM

3 ROLL AND STRETCH THE STRUDEL DOUGH

4 FILL AND BAKE THE STRUDEL

1 MAKE THE STRUDEL DOUGH

1 Sift the flour onto the work surface and make a well in the centre. In a bowl, beat the egg to mix with the water, lemon juice, and a pinch of salt and pour into the well.

2 Work the ingredients in the well, drawing in a little of the flour with your fingertips.

3 Gradually draw in the remaining flour with the palette knife, continuing to work the flour in with your fingertips. Gently knead in just enough flour so that the dough forms a ball; it should be quite soft.

4 Flour the work surface and knead the dough 5-7 minutes, picking it up and throwing it down, until shiny and smooth. Shape into a ball, cover with a bowl, and let rest 30 minutes. Meanwhile, prepare the filling.

ANNE SAYS
"Thorough kneading is critical for creating an elastic dough. Alternatively, work the dough in an electric mixer with the dough hook."

Kneading dough thoroughly makes it elastic

Dough will "relax" while it sits and will be easier to stretch

2 PREPARE THE FILLING AND CHANTILLY CREAM

1 Stone all the cherries (see box, page 116). Grate the zest from the lemon onto the plate.

2 Using the chef's knife, coarsely chop the walnuts.

ANNE SAYS
"Nuts are best chopped by hand to control the finished texture although this will always be uneven."

3 To make the Chantilly cream, pour the cream into a chilled bowl and whip until soft peaks form. Add the sugar and brandy or vanilla essence and continue whipping until the cream forms stiff peaks and the whisk leaves clear marks in the cream. Chill.

3 ROLL AND STRETCH THE STRUDEL DOUGH

1 Cover the work table with the bed sheet and lightly flour it. Roll out the dough to as large a square as possible. Cover it with the damp tea towel and let rest about 15 minutes. Heat the oven to 190°C (375°F, Gas 5) and butter the baking sheet. Melt the butter in the small saucepan.

Flour your hands from time to time while stretching dough

Any small holes that appear will not show when the dough is rolled up

2 Flour your hands and place them under the dough. Starting at the centre and working outwards, carefully stretch the dough with the backs of both hands. Continue to work outwards as the dough gets thinner, gently lifting and flopping it on the surface. It should be as large a square as possible.

3 At once, brush the dough thoroughly with about three-quarters of the melted butter.

! TAKE CARE !
The stretched dough dries quickly and becomes brittle.

HOW TO STONE CHERRIES

Choose firm cherries with shiny skin; avoid any with a dry stalk.

To stone with a cherry stoner: this convenient tool pushes the stone through the fruit, leaving a full hollow. As a result, more of the cherry juices will be released when the cherries are cooked.

To stone with a vegetable peeler: insert the tip of the peeler in the stalk end, rotate around the stone, and scoop it out. The result will be neater than with a cherry stoner, and more juice will be retained.

4 FILL AND BAKE THE STRUDEL

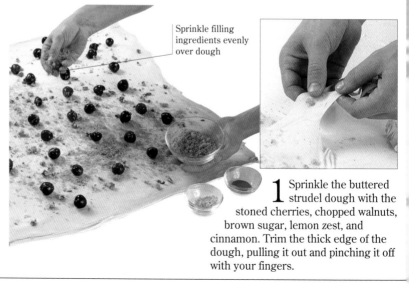

Sprinkle filling ingredients evenly over dough

1 Sprinkle the buttered strudel dough with the stoned cherries, chopped walnuts, brown sugar, lemon zest, and cinnamon. Trim the thick edge of the dough, pulling it out and pinching it off with your fingers.

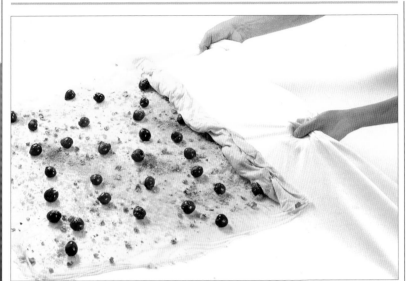

DRIED FRUIT STRUDEL

When fresh cherries are not in season, try this dried fruit version of Cherry Strudel.

Use wide pastry brush to apply melted butter

2 Roll up the strudel with the help of the sheet. Transfer the roll to the prepared baking sheet and shape it into a crescent.

3 Brush the strudel with the remaining melted butter and bake in the heated oven until the skewer inserted in the centre of the strudel for 30 seconds is hot when withdrawn, 30-40 minutes. The strudel should be crisp and golden brown.

1 Coarsely chop 500 g (1 lb) mixed dried fruit (apricots, prunes, dates, raisins, figs), discarding any stones. Put in a small pan, cover with 125 ml (4 fl oz) dark rum and 125 ml (4 fl oz) water, and heat gently, stirring occasionally, about 5 minutes. Take from the heat and leave until cool and all the fruit is plump.
2 Meanwhile, make the Chantilly cream as directed, flavouring it with vanilla essence or rum.
3 Drain the fruit thoroughly, discarding the liquid.
4 Prepare and stretch the strudel dough as directed in the main recipe; brush with melted butter.
5 Sprinkle the dough with the dried fruit, chopped walnuts, brown sugar, and cinnamon; omit the lemon zest.
6 Roll and bake as directed. Serve with the Chantilly cream.

¡❂¡ TO SERVE
Sprinkle the strudel with icing sugar and serve hot or cold, with the Chantilly cream.

Fresh cherries add a pretty touch

Pastry is deliciously light and flaky

HAZELNUT TORTE WITH STRAWBERRIES

 SERVES 8   WORK TIME 40-45 MINUTES*   BAKING TIME 15-18 MINUTES

EQUIPMENT

pastry scraper

piping bag and star nozzle

whisk**

rubber spatula

cling film

chef's knife

bowl sieve

small ladle

small knife

palette knife

conical sieve

tea towel

3 baking sheets

2 wire racks

bowls

food processor***

20 cm (8 inch) saucepan lid

**electric mixer can also be used
***blender can also be used

An impressive three-layer castle of hazelnut pastry sandwiched with strawberries and whipped cream. A tart raspberry coulis is an ideal accompaniment.

GETTING AHEAD

The pastry rounds can be baked 1-2 days ahead and kept in an airtight container or can be frozen. The torte can be assembled up to 4 hours ahead and refrigerated.

*plus 30-60 minutes chilling time

metric	SHOPPING LIST	imperial
750 g	strawberries	1¹/₂ lb
	fresh mint sprigs for decoration	
	For the hazelnut pastry	
250 g	hazelnuts	8 oz
135 g	caster sugar	4¹/₂ oz
125 g	plain flour	4 oz
2.5 ml	salt	¹/₂ tsp
150 g	unsalted butter	5 oz
1	egg yolk	1
	For the raspberry coulis	
500 g	fresh or drained defrosted raspberries	1 lb
30-45 ml	icing sugar	2-3 tbsp
15-30 ml	kirsch (optional)	1-2 tbsp
	For the Chantilly cream	
375 ml	double cream	12 fl oz
22.5 ml	caster sugar	1¹/₂ tbsp
5 ml	vanilla essence	1 tsp

INGREDIENTS

hazelnuts

strawberries

raspberries

icing sugar

egg yolk

fresh mint

unsalted butter

double cream

plain flour

vanilla essence

kirsch (optional)

caster sugar

ORDER OF WORK

1 MAKE THE HAZELNUT PASTRY DOUGH

2 SHAPE AND BAKE THE HAZELNUT PASTRY LAYERS

3 MAKE THE COULIS AND CHANTILLY CREAM; ASSEMBLE THE TORTE

1 MAKE THE HAZELNUT PASTRY DOUGH

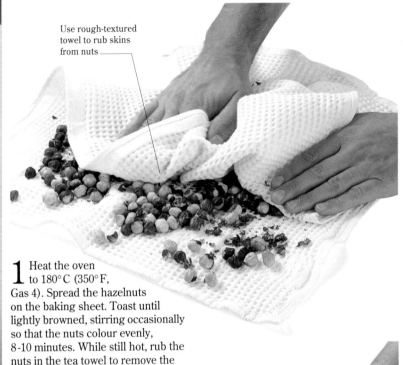

Use rough-textured towel to rub skins from nuts

2 In the food processor, grind the hazelnuts with the caster sugar to a fine powder.

ANNE SAYS
"If using a blender, grind the nuts and sugar in 2-3 batches."

1 Heat the oven to 180°C (350°F, Gas 4). Spread the hazelnuts on the baking sheet. Toast until lightly browned, stirring occasionally so that the nuts colour evenly, 8-10 minutes. While still hot, rub the nuts in the tea towel to remove the skins, then leave to cool.

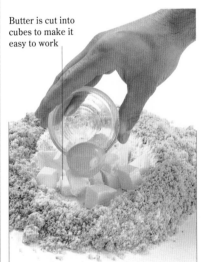

Butter is cut into cubes to make it easy to work

Mix quickly – using your fingertips only – for a light result

3 Put the ground nut mixture on the work surface and sift the flour and salt on top. Make a well in the centre of the ingredients and add the butter and egg yolk.

4 Using your fingertips, work the butter and egg yolk together in the well, drawing in a little of the ground nut and flour mixtures, until soft and thoroughly mixed.

5 Draw in the nut and flour mixture with the pastry scraper, working them into the butter mixture with your fingers until combined. Press the dough into a ball.

6 Sprinkle the work surface lightly with flour; place the dough on the work surface and blend the dough by pushing it away from you with the heel of your hand.

ANNE SAYS
"The dough will be quite sticky."

Dough is ready to chill

7 Gather up the dough with the pastry scraper and continue to blend gently until it is very smooth in texture.

8 Shape the dough into a ball, wrap it tightly, and chill until firm, at least 30 minutes.

! TAKE CARE !
Pastry doughs made with nuts are particularly delicate. Be sure to give the dough enough time to chill.

2 SHAPE AND BAKE THE HAZELNUT PASTRY LAYERS

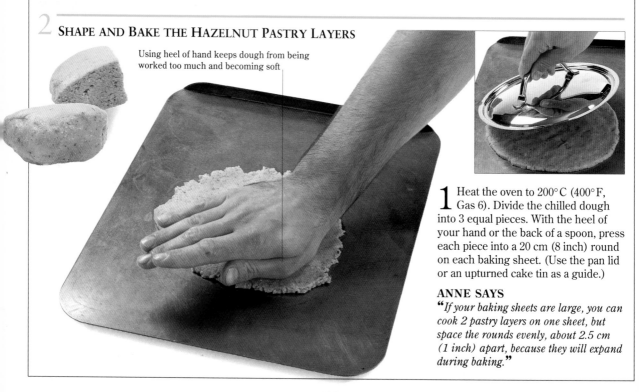

Using heel of hand keeps dough from being worked too much and becoming soft

1 Heat the oven to 200°C (400°F, Gas 6). Divide the chilled dough into 3 equal pieces. With the heel of your hand or the back of a spoon, press each piece into a 20 cm (8 inch) round on each baking sheet. (Use the pan lid or an upturned cake tin as a guide.)

ANNE SAYS
"If your baking sheets are large, you can cook 2 pastry layers on one sheet, but space the rounds evenly, about 2.5 cm (1 inch) apart, because they will expand during baking."

Lay pastry flat on wire rack so it keeps its shape when cooled

2 Bake the pastry layers in the heated oven until the edges begin to brown, 15-18 minutes. While they are still warm, trim them with the chef's knife to neat rounds using the pan lid as a guide.

! TAKE CARE !
Do not let the pastry cool before trimming or the rounds may break.

3 Using the chef's knife, cut one of the pastry layers all the way across into 8 equal wedges. Let all the layers and the wedges cool to tepid on the baking sheets.

4 Using the palette knife, carefully transfer the pastry triangles and rounds from the baking sheets to the wire racks to cool completely.

ANNE SAYS
"If the rounds stick, warm them on the baking sheets in the oven, 2-3 minutes, to loosen them from the sheets."

3 MAKE THE COULIS AND CHANTILLY CREAM; ASSEMBLE THE TORTE

Point of small knife lifts out hulls

1 To make the raspberry coulis, pick over the berries, then purée them in the food processor. Stir in icing sugar to taste, and the kirsch, if you like. Work the purée through the conical sieve to remove the pips.

2 Hull the strawberries, washing them only if they are dirty. Set aside 8 small berries for decoration. Halve the remaining strawberries, or quarter them if they are large.

! TAKE CARE !
Washing softens strawberries, so only wash them if absolutely necessary.

3 To make the Chantilly cream, pour the cream into a chilled bowl and whip until soft peaks form. Add the sugar and vanilla essence and continue whipping until the cream forms stiff peaks and the whisk leaves clear marks in the cream. Spoon about one-quarter of the cream into the piping bag.

4 Set one round of pastry on a serving plate. Cover with about one-quarter of the remaining Chantilly cream, and arrange half of the strawberries on top.

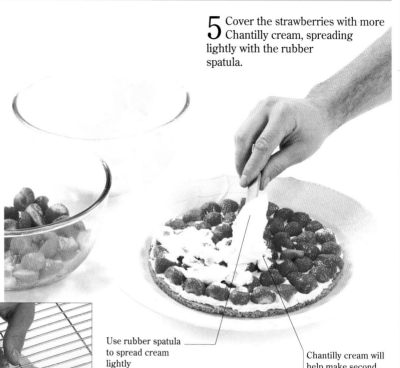

5 Cover the strawberries with more Chantilly cream, spreading lightly with the rubber spatula.

Use rubber spatula to spread cream lightly

Chantilly cream will help make second pastry round stick when placed on top

6 Set the second round of pastry on top and spread with half of the remaining Chantilly cream.

ANNE SAYS
"Slide the pastry round directly from the wire rack to avoid breaking it."

7 Cover with the remaining strawberries and carefully spread the rest of the Chantilly cream on top, smoothing it gently.

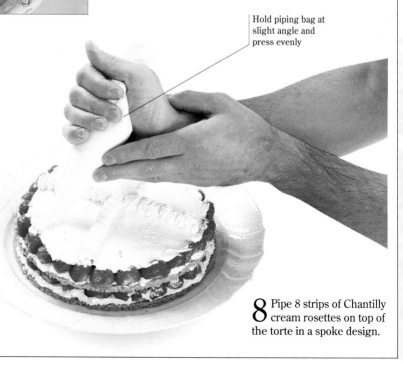

Hold piping bag at slight angle and press evenly

8 Pipe 8 strips of Chantilly cream rosettes on top of the torte in a spoke design.

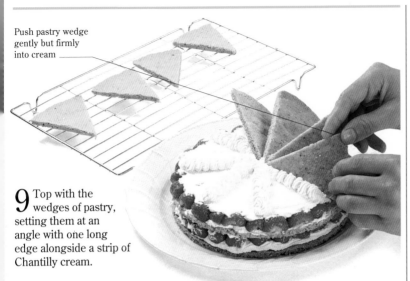

Push pastry wedge gently but firmly into cream

9 Top with the wedges of pastry, setting them at an angle with one long edge alongside a strip of Chantilly cream.

10 Put a whole strawberry in the gaps between the pastry wedges. Pipe a large swirled rosette of Chantilly cream in the centre of the torte. Strip the mint leaves from the sprigs and use them to decorate the torte.

🍽 **TO SERVE**

Cut between the pastry wedges. Serve the raspberry coulis separately.

Mint leaves are bright, fresh colour contrast

Crisp hazelnut pastry wedges are irresistible with whipped cream and strawberries

FRUIT KNOW-HOW

Home-grown fruit beats all others. Depending on the location and climate, if you have your own trees you can enjoy the exceptional flavour of the fruit for at least a brief season in the year. Small farm shops embody this principle and often carry produce that is exceptional because it is locally picked and tree-ripened. They may also offer more varieties of fruit than can be found in larger stores and supermarkets.

CHOOSING FRUIT

Modern technology has brought considerable changes to the production of fruit. It is tempting to condemn this, given inferior flavour and the increasing use of chemical sprays. But these changes are counter-balanced by huge benefits: our favourite fruit can be eaten year-round instead of being a seasonal treat, and the most exotic fruit may appear in your local supermarkets.

It is important to know how to choose fruit at the market. The biggest and brightest fruit is not necessarily the best – in fact, probably far from it! Here are some tips on what to look for when buying specific types of fruit.

Apples: firm and bright with an even background colour; no bruises (but brown patches, or russeting, do not mean poor quality). *Pears:* firm, but yielding slightly at the stalk end, with the stalk still attached. *Peaches and nectarines:* firm but not hard, with a yellow or cream-coloured background and a distinct seam along the side; no greenish tinge, bruises, or wrinkled or shrivelled skin (brown patches signal decay). *Apricots:* should give when pressed; soft velvety skin with no greenish tinge. *Plums:* uniform in colour with smooth skin and slightly soft flesh. *Cherries:* plump, shiny, and well-coloured with green, not dark or dry, stalks. *Lemons and limes:* smooth skin that is not shrivelled. *Oranges:* firm with no blemishes. *Grapefruit:* resilient, with no soft patches. (All citrus fruit should feel heavy with juice.) *Green, red, and black grapes:* unblemished and of uniform colour, firmly attached to the stalk; good aroma. Red and black grapes should not have a greenish tinge. *Strawberries:* uniform colour and moist green hull; perfumed aroma.

Raspberries, blackberries, boysenberries, and other soft berries: plump with brilliant-to-deep colour; no mould or rot. *Blueberries and other firm berries:* plump and shiny, with deep colour. (Always buy berries in small containers because those in large containers may be crushed by their own weight.) *Dessert melons, such as honeydew, cantaloupe, Charentais, and Gallia:* heavy for their size and firm, with no soft spots, cracks, or mould; a heady aroma with no rotting overtones. *Watermelons:* deep green, matt skin; shake small ones because loose seeds indicate ripeness. *Bananas:* fairly soft skin when ripe, possibly with brown spots; no black patches. *Pineapples:* large and heavy with sweet aroma and central leaves that can be pulled out from the plume. *Mangoes:* a sweet smell and taut skin with no soft spots. *Papayas:* small, with deep colour. *Kiwi fruit:* should yield slightly, with no soft spots. *Passion fruit:* dry shrivelled skin and heavy for its size. *Pomegranates:* large and heavy in your hand, with clean skin. *Persimmons:* bright orange when ripe, with soft yielding pulp. *Star fruit or carambola:* firm, with juicy flesh. *Lychees:* unbroken bumpy skin, pink to brownish in colour. *Purple and green figs:* dry with a sweet odour and no blemishes.

FRUIT AND YOUR HEALTH

With health concerns on the rise, many cooks turn to fruit desserts for their high vitamin content and low calories. Several of the recipes in **Fruit Desserts** are naturally healthy, containing little or no butter, eggs, double cream, or sugar. Summer Fruit Salad and Mango Sorbet are two delicious examples. And with the simple modifications suggested here, other, richer fruit desserts can be made healthier and less fattening so that you can enjoy a balance between taste and nutrition.

The sugar in every recipe can be reduced according to taste, and polyunsaturated margarine can be substituted for butter (although pastry recipes will suffer in taste and texture). You can omit Chantilly cream accompaniments and decorations: Pear and Redcurrant Compote, Baked Peaches with Amaretti, and Cherry Strudel lighten up considerably when you leave out the whipped cream on the side. Make fruit tartlets and tarts without the pastry cream, and serve soufflé puddings without the custard sauce – and you're on your way to making desserts that are healthier but just as pleasurable.

If you have a specific health problem, consult your doctor and follow his recommended diet.

CLEANING FRUIT

Fruit that is eaten with its skin may be washed gently in cold or warm water but should never be left to soak or it will become soggy. Water also encourages rotting in soft fruit, so avoid washing delicate fruit such as berries unless they are very sandy. Some fruit, such as apples and citrus fruit, may be preserved with an edible wax; this can usually be removed by scrubbing the fruit under running water. Most modern pesticides used on fruit cannot be eliminated by washing; however, peeling fruit will reduce contamination.

PREVENTING DISCOLORATION

When exposed to air, certain tannins and enzymes in fruit such as apples, peaches, and pears react, turning the cut fruit brown. Acid helps prevent this: rub the cut surfaces of the fruit with a halved lemon or lime, or immerse the fruit in water mixed with a little lemon or lime juice (this is called "acidulation"). Always peel or cut these fruit with a stainless steel knife because other metals may encourage discoloration. Fruit that discolours should be prepared as quickly as possible, just before it is needed.

STORING FRUIT

The type of fruit, and how ripe it is when you buy it, determines how long it can be kept. Some fruit, such as apples, pears, and oranges, ripen relatively slowly. Others – grapes and berries, for example – become ripe or overripe within a few days of maturity and cannot be stored for long. Fully ripened fruit should be refrigerated immediately. Discard any overripe or mouldy pieces – berries are particularly susceptible to mould. Handle fruit gently because bruising or crushing encourages rot.

If a piece of fruit needs to ripen further at home, keep it at room temperature. It will ripen more quickly if wrapped, so store the fruit in a brown paper bag punctured with holes. If the fruit is extremely hard, the process can be accelerated by adding a very ripe piece of fruit to the bag. Some fruit, such as apples, nectarines, berries, and pears, will rot if left with their skins touching. If ripening them for more than a day, spread them out or wrap them individually in paper.

HOW-TO BOXES

*There are pictures of all preparation steps for each **Fruit Desserts** recipe. Some basic techniques are general to a number of recipes; they are shown in extra detail in these special "how-to" boxes.*

INDEX